GEOFF NICHOLSON is the author of more than twenty books, which have been widely translated with one made into a Hollywood film. These include the acclaimed novel *Bleeding London* (shortlisted for the Whitbread Prize), as well as the classics of psychogeographical non-fiction, *The Lost Art of Walking* and *Walking in Ruins*. Nicholson has written for the *Guardian*, *Telegraph* and *New York Times*, and is currently a contributing editor to the *Los Angeles Review of Books*. He lives in Essex.

www.geoffnicholsonwriter.com

ALSO BY GEOFF NICHOLSON

Fiction

Street Sleeper
The Knot Garden
What We Did on Our Holidays
Hunters and Gatherers
The Food Chain
The Errol Flynn Novel
Still Life with Volkswagens
Everything and More
Footsucker
Bleeding London
Flesh Guitar
Female Ruins
Bedlam Burning
The Hollywood Dodo
Gravity's Volkswagen
The City Under the Skin
The Miranda

Non-Fiction

Big Noises
Day Trips to the Desert
Andy Warhol: A Beginner's Guide
Frank Lloyd Wright: A Beginner's Guide
Sex Collectors
The Lost Art of Walking
Walking in Ruins
The London Complaint
The Suburbanist

WALKING ON THIN AIR

A Life's Journey in 99 Steps

GEOFF NICHOLSON

The Westbourne Press

THE WESTBOURNE PRESS
An Imprint of Saqi Books
Gable House, 18–24 Turnham Green Terrace, London W4 1QP
www.westbournepress.co.uk
www.saqibooks.com

Published 2023 by The Westbourne Press

A full CIP record for this book is available from the British Library.

ISBN 978 1 908906 57 1
eISBN 978 1 908906 58 8

Printed and bound in Great Britain by Clays Ltd, Elcograf S.p.A

'I walk slowly, like one who comes from so far away he doesn't expect to arrive.'

JORGE LUIS BORGES

1

This is a short book about walking and mortality. I like to say that I've walked all my life. I know that can't be literally true since there was obviously a time when I was too young to do any walking at all but, according to my mother, I started walking very early and I haven't stopped since. I'll continue as long as I can, but being mortal, I know that sooner or later I'll stop, that there will be a last step for me, a last excursion, a final drift, just as there is for everybody. All things good and bad, and that includes living and walking, must come to an end. Would we really want it any other way?

2

I'm a walker who writes and a writer who walks. I've never been one of those 'sacramental' or 'spiritual' walkers like Bruce Chatwin or Peace Pilgrim (born Mildred Lisette Norman), much as I admire them, and I'm not one of those 'stunt' walkers, walking backwards across America, like Patrick Harmon in 1915, or walking 1000 miles in 1000 consecutive hours, like Captain Barclay in 1809. I'm not exactly a psychogeographic walker like Guy Debord or Iain Sinclair or Will Self or Rachel Lichtenstein or Teju Cole, though I do a lot of the things that psychogeographers do, which is also to do a lot of the things that flâneurs do, though I don't claim to be a Baudelaire. I do what I do. I go to places, I walk when I'm there, I look around, I write about what I see and feel. It's not the only thing I do with my life, but it's probably the best part.

My life hasn't been especially nomadic. I've lived for long periods in Sheffield, London and Los Angeles, with occasional short spells living in Cambridge, Colchester, Halifax and New York. I'm currently living, for one reason and another, in semi-urban Essex. As a tourist or working writer, I've found myself in Munich, Berlin, Paris, Guadalajara, Alice Springs, Tokyo, as well as in various deserts – the Sahara, the Australian Outback, several American deserts. Wherever I've been, I've walked, and in some cases I've gone to places specifically to walk and then write about them. It's a life, and sometimes, more often than you might think and very much to my surprise, it's a living.

3

The majority of my walking has been done in what we might call the built environment, in cities rather than in nature, though as that list suggests, I also love deserts, and my favourite, the one where I've spent most time and done the most walking, is the Mojave, just a couple of hours from Los Angeles. In fact, its proximity to the desert was one of the things that first attracted me to LA.

The Mojave contains Death Valley, one of the great places on earth, and I especially love walking there. I'd enjoy it more if there were fewer other visitors, but if fewer people visited, there wouldn't be guided trails, signposts and a ranger station. The risk of death would be considerably higher.

A few years back I was walking by the Ubehebe Crater, (pronounced you-be, he-be) a half-mile-wide, seven-hundred-foot-deep cavity, created by the coming together of magma and ground water. The name, which may come from the Paiute or the Timbisha Shoshone language, is generally accepted to mean big basket or coyote's basket.

I was not rash enough or intrepid enough to walk all the way to the bottom of the crater and back up again, but I decided to walk around the rim, which is a reasonable excursion, and described by the National Park Service as 'moderately difficult due to the initial climb and loose footing.'

Moderate difficulty I could cope with, or thought I could. In fact, I'd done the walk a few years earlier and found it fairly comfortable, but on this second occasion I found it very hard work indeed. I didn't give up because you can't when you're halfway round the rim of a volcanic crater. But by the end I was exhausted, really suffering, sweating, heart pounding, painfully gasping for breath.

I didn't think too much about it at the time. I accepted my tiredness and lack of puff as just another wretched symptom of getting older. But a little while later I went for one of my regular medical checkups in LA, and the doctor was concerned about my red blood cell count. It was low, not dangerously so, he said, but we needed to keep an eye on it, which we did.

A couple of years later, a different doctor in a different country, England, decided that my blood cell count was now indeed dangerously low. And after a variety of tests, he was able to put a name to my condition: CMML – Chronic Myelomonocytic Leukemia, a cancer of the bone marrow, that being the place where blood cells are made. CMML is sometimes described in the literature as a 'rare type of blood cancer' – not rare enough, obviously. And made even less desirable when I learned that Silvio Berlusconi also shared the condition.

Its origins seem to be genetic, a mutation of a chromosome, so none of this was my fault, not caused by my bad habits and less than healthy lifestyle, but it was serious. I was told it was treatable, but not curable. The treatment started out with occasional blood transfusions, then moved on to weekly injections of EPO, the regime I'm currently following. EPO – erythropoietin – is a hormone which stimulates red blood cell production and allows the blood to carry more oxygen. This has all kinds of benefits, not least for walking. It's also the stuff that elite cyclists use when they want to cheat.

The prognosis is not great. At some point the leukemia will change from chronic to acute, and this can happen after months or after a couple of decades. This is very bad news, a death sentence according to some opinions. At that point, a bone marrow transplant is an option, but not one I think I'll be taking. As I write this, a few years after my initial diagnosis, I feel pretty good most days. I get tired sometimes, more often than I used to, but doesn't everybody? And of course, I continue to walk.

4

Once every three months or so I go to see a consultant at the hospital in Colchester, which is close to where I now live. I usually travel there by train, which requires me to make a fifteen-minute walk up quite a steep hill from the station to the hospital. It's not punishing by Ubehebe Crater standards but it's a proper hill. You can work up a sweat, you breathe hard along the way; or at least I do. Nevertheless, my continuing ability to walk up the hill seems to impress the doctors. I feel oddly comforted by this. Sooner or later, I suppose things will change, walking will become much more difficult and walking up that hill will eventually be impossible. For now, however, I carry on walking because it's what I do, what I've always done. And I continue to write and read and think and talk about it, and if much of my interest seems arty or literary or bookish, well, that's who I am.

I wouldn't say that intimations of mortality and potential immobility have put a spring in my step, but they have concentrated my mind. Every walk, any walk, now seems just a little more intense, a little more urgent, than it used to. I concentrate more, think more, feel more. Some walkers might describe this as mindfulness. I prefer to think of it as business as usual, even though I know it isn't, not really.

5

I get a bit weary of being told about the multiple health benefits of walking. I regularly read or hear how good walking is for maintaining a healthy weight, increasing heart and lung capability, strengthening bones and muscles, building up stamina, preventing high blood pressure, high cholesterol and type 2 diabetes. I've read that it's good for easing knee, hip and back pain, warding off dementia, improving sleep, boosting immunity and energy, even increasing the chances of getting pregnant.

I don't doubt that most, perhaps all, of this is true, but being 'good for you' and 'causing improvements' suggests there's a measurable baseline, and I'm never sure there really is. You end up saying something like, however bad you are, you'll be worse if you don't walk. Who would argue?

I've never been a true invalid, I've never been a spectacularly healthy specimen, and we could argue about what that even means, but I won't. Suffice it to say that being a walker and being unhealthy, are not mutually exclusive, but no doubt I'd have been less healthy if I'd done less walking.

I also often hear that it's best to walk in a 'natural' environment, but increasingly I don't know what a natural environment is. Is it a park? A wood? A place designated as an 'Area of Outstanding Natural Beauty'? Well maybe, I actually live in one of those AONBs at the moment, but this is an official government classification, and that seems to me only natural in a very specific limited sense. How about a mangrove swamp? A pitiless tract of desert? A volcano? These are all natural, aren't they? Just how natural do you want? How good is it to walk in those places?

However, even if all the professed physical benefits are absolutely true, that has very little to do with why I walk. I walk because I want to, because I like it, and I know that I'll be miserable if age and decay prevent me from walking. For that reason, I'm much more persuaded that walking is good for mental health. Here the literature will tell you that walking is good for reducing stress, depression and anxiety. I can attest that in my own case walking does a world of good for all these things, especially depression. I often walk to cheer myself up.

It's also said that walking is good for 'creative thinking'. Again, I'm not absolutely sure what that term means, but I've certainly had one or two good ideas while out walking. Could I have had these, or similar ideas, sitting at a desk or lying in bed or while propping up a bar? Maybe, maybe not, but I have no idea what experiment you could possibly conduct to prove or disprove any of this.

6

I'm far more comfortable with the idea of walking as a form of meditation. I don't get into a fugue state when I walk, but often, especially at the beginning of a walk, I feel much more alert, more perceptive, much more interested and involved in what I'm seeing and doing. This applies just as much when I'm walking in nature as when I'm walking in an inner city. By some definitions, this might, I suppose, be called 'mindfulness'.

There are various kinds of more formal walking meditation, often deriving from Buddhism, known as *kinhin* in Japanese. There's circumambulation, the act of walking around a sacred space. But I always think of John Cage who, in an interview with a journalist, was asked about sacred mushrooms, and he was having none of it, and he said he rejected the idea of some things being sacred and some things not. I profoundly agree with this to be true. Admittedly I would in general prefer to walk in the Peak District than through the nearby industrial estate, but I'm not averse to walking through industrial estates, and true enlightenment might not even recognise the difference.

There's some slight evidence that Qigong, a form of walking, breathing, meditation and martial art, has some effect in increasing the death of cancer cells. There's far more general evidence that walking is some help for some kinds of cancer. The Journal of Cancer Survivorship publishes a lot of articles suggesting that pretty much any kind of exercise improves survival rates for cancer sufferers, but few cancer sufferers are going to be kickboxing and windsurfing. Walking is the one we tend to go for.

7

In the end, we may all be prepared to agree that walking is a good thing. However, contrarian that I am, I keep a scrapbook containing cuttings of all the terrible things that can and do happen to people while walking: being mowed down by cars or motorcycles, bikes or electric scooters, in one case by an ambulance. Walkers get mugged, they get lost in the wilderness, they're attacked by bees and dogs and cows and bears and even other walkers. People fall into ditches, or off cliff edges; they fall down manholes while texting. They die by inhaling the 'bloom' of toxic algae. In extreme cases, walkers are hit by a stray bullet or killed by treading on a landmine or by being stabbed to death by a motiveless lunatic.

I try not to be too morbid about it, and I never take pleasure in other people's misery. Chiefly I do it to remind myself, and others, that walking is not an entirely tame, easy, altogether safe activity. We walkers take some comfort in risk.

8

Neville Cardus (1888–1975) is widely regarded as one of the greatest cricket writers there's ever been. He was a dandy both in his prose style and his life. He used to carry an ebony walking stick, but only for ornamental purposes. He didn't need it for walking; he needed it to *pose*.

Cardus listed walking as one of his hobbies, and he did come up with one of the great observations about walking and physical decay. He said that the body ages but the mind doesn't. 'I want to go for an eight-mile walk. My mind goes for an eight-mile walk. My damn legs won't go.'

When I first read that I didn't know what on earth he was talking about, but now I understand all too well.

9

Jorge Luis Borges was a collector of walking sticks. He needed them, of course, because towards the end of his life he was blind. Sources differ on when he completely lost his sight, but it seems to have been around the age of fifty-five. From then on he used a stick and needed somebody to help him walk. And he never learned braille, so he also needed somebody to help him read, or at least read to him. I'm not sure whether walking or reading would have been the greater loss, but Borges never seems to have had much trouble finding people to help him with either activity. All manner of people – Alberto Manguel, Norman di Giovanni and Robert Robinson among them – went to visit him, walked with him and read to him. Some, I'm sure, gave him a walking stick or two to add to his collection.

Borges's poem 'Things' describes the objects he possesses, the ones that will still be around after he's died. First on the list of things is his walking stick, or cane depending on the translation.

Borges was extremely quotable on the subject of walking: 'Which one of us has never felt, walking through the twilight or writing down a date from his past, that he has lost something infinite?'

Infinity: in the end I think that was Borges's chief subject. It's a tricky one for a walker, because all walks by definition are finite. You may not know how far you're going to walk or where you'll end up, but there's always an end; you can't walk forever.

At the very end of his life, Borges was living in Geneva but still had an apartment in Buenos Aires. Knowing he was in bad health and with not long to live, he tried to arrange to sell the Buenos Aires property and have its contents shipped to Geneva, but he ran into trouble with his nephew, his sister's son. The nephew claimed that the apartment belonged jointly to Borges and his sister. You'd think there must surely have been some legal documents that clarified the position one way or another, but apparently not. More complicated was the matter of the contents, especially about who owned some silverware and a chiffonier that had belonged to the Borges grandmother. The dispute was an ugly one, however, among the things over which there was no dispute were Borges' books and his walking sticks.

10

There's an interview Tom Waits did with Terry Gross on National Public Radio in which she asked him whether, when he started listening to 'older music' it affected the way he dressed or spoke or behaved. Waits replied that it did. He bought an old hat and an old car, and he sported a walking stick.

Gross interrupted to ask what kind of walking cane it was, did it have a silver top? 'No, no,' said Waits, 'an old man's cane from a Salvation Army. Yeah … It gave me a walk, I guess. It just gave me something I liked identity-wise.'

A walking stick may well give you an identity, but you have to ask yourself whether it's the identity you want. In the years right before she died, Queen Elizabeth used a 'thumb stick,' longer and sturdier than an ordinary walking stick, keeping the walker more upright, good for the posture and good for preventing back ache. In some parts of the world, including the Cairngorms, these are known as snake sticks, the idea being that should you encounter an adder on your walk you simply turn the stick upside down and the handle fits snuggly around the snake's head. I imagine this isn't a problem the queen had to deal with.

11

There was a time, a good few years back, long before my cancer diagnosis, when I was suffering from all kinds of problems with my left leg. I'd wake up on certain mornings and I'd be completely unable to walk. I'd be crippled for three or four days, then it would pass, and it was as though nothing had happened. It was hard to live with, but it was even harder to find a doctor who could identify what I was suffering from. I was diagnosed as having tendonitis, bursitis, plantar fasciitis – all good names, and all of which essentially mean that you've got a pain in your leg. Putting a name to the condition helped a little, but I couldn't find a doctor able to cure it.

Eventually, when I was living in Los Angeles, I went to see a doctor who specialised in these kinds of problems, and he came highly recommended. In fact, mounted on the wall of his waiting room were endorsements from Brian Wilson of the Beach Boys and Shirley MacLaine. These were wildly enthusiastic and laudatory, but it occurred to me that they both had a lot more money to throw around than I did and, given that they both had a reputation for, shall we say, eccentricity, their endorsement might not be completely applicable to my own situation.

Eventually I got in to see the doctor. He had me take my shoes off and walk up and down the office while he watched. After about fifteen seconds he concluded that what I needed was a pair of orthotics, the kind he specialised in, one for each foot, which would cost $500 each. I fled the office.

Another time, when I was having a particularly bad spell, I asked my wife to buy me a walking stick. She found a place on Hollywood Boulevard that sold walking sticks with a spider set in the Lucite handle. She bought me one of those. It looked fantastic and it was a lot of help in getting around.

And then after I'd had the stick for a couple of days, I realised the top screwed off, the cane was hollow and there was a swordstick concealed inside. That made it even more fantastic. It seemed like the kind of cane Tom Waits or Borges ought to have used, and I could certainly see the attractions of walking along with a cane that contained a spider and a concealed weapon.

It was the kind of affectation a man might get used to. But I gave it up once my foot got better. I didn't want to use the stick as part of a pose (unlike Neville Cardus). I reckoned that one day I might really need a cane full-time, and I didn't want to bring on that day by using one before I needed to.

And then I found the right doctor. I thought she seemed a bit flakey, a bit New Age and hippyish, but after a talk and some blood tests she concluded that I was probably suffering from gout, that classic and rather shameful disease, supposedly the province of old soaks and port drinkers. This was in fact something that had already occurred to me, but the symptoms had never been absolutely right and even this new doctor said the amount of uric acid in my blood, the stuff that causes gout, wasn't all that high. But she reckoned I should start taking one pill of allopurinol every day and see what happened. I've done it ever since and haven't had a single gout attack.

It occurs to me sometimes that maybe I didn't have gout, or perhaps I used to have it and it's simply gone away, or the medication may just be a placebo. But what does it matter? The diagnosis and the daily allopurinol have enabled me to walk. I don't use a walking stick, at least not yet, but I have one in reserve, with a silver handle in the shape of a skull. It sits by my desk waiting for the moment when it will be needed.

12

After the gout had been diagnosed, I was sitting in the waiting room of my GP's office, on the outskirts of Beverly Hills, when a huge man walked in. It was, I realised after a moment, Lou Ferrigno, star of *The Incredible Hulk*, and who appeared as a most unlikely neighbour in *The King of Queens*. Of course, this being Los Angeles, no celebrity ever has to do anything so undignified as sitting in a waiting room with the masses, so he was immediately sent through to see the doctor ahead of me.

When it was, at last, my turn to see the doctor I went in and said, 'So, Lou Ferrigno? Does he suffer from gout too?' Because frankly, given the way he walked, I thought he might.

My doctor smiled enigmatically and said, 'I can't tell you what Lou is suffering from, but I can tell you it's not gout.'

I suppose this could pass for doctor/patient privilege.

13

There's a strange and wonderful short story by Rudyard Kipling, first published in 1885, titled 'The City of Dreadful Night'. There's also a poem with the same title by James 'B.V.' Thomson, published a few years earlier. Both works are about walking through a city at night. Thomson's city was London: Kipling's was Lahore.

Kipling knew Lahore. After he'd failed to get into Oxford on a scholarship, his father got him a job as assistant editor on a Lahore newspaper, *The Civil and Military Gazette*. That's where the short story was first published. It's about a man who, unable to sleep on a stiflingly hot night, goes for a nocturnal walk around Lahore.

As he walks, he sees people asleep in the streets looking like corpses, and he sees real corpses pushing up out of the ground in a 'disused Mahomedan burial-ground.'

The narrator enters the Wazir Khan Mosque,

climbs a tower, hears the call of the muezzin and, as he descends, encounters men carrying something. 'What is it? Something borne on men's shoulders comes by in the half-light, and I stand back. A woman's corpse going down to the burning-ghat, and a bystander tells him that she died from the heat. 'So,' our narrator concludes, 'the city was of Death as well as Night after all.'

In fact, I think we, and he, might have guessed that. When our walker is about to set out on his walk, he's not sure which direction to head in. Here's where the walking stick comes in. He stands in the middle of his garden, sets his walking stick upright, lets go and waits to see how it falls, and that's the direction he'll walk. In the event it points down a moonlit road leading to 'The City of Dreadful Night.'

Choosing a direction in which to start walking can sometimes be a difficult decision, but I suspect that a lot of people, if they knew that one possible direction led to a place known as The City of Dreadful Night, might decide to take another route, any other route. On the other hand, some, regardless of where the stick fell, might have headed in precisely that direction. Some people choose to walk away from death, some have no choice.

14

Another walking stick user was Virginia Woolf. She committed suicide in March 1941 by walking into the River Ouse in Rodmell, Sussex, next to the house where she was then living with husband Leonard. She left him a note that said, 'You have given me the greatest possible happiness ... I don't think two people could have been happier till this terrible disease came.' I wonder if he believed that. I'm not sure that I do, but it was a very nice thing to say. Given how close the Woolf house was to the river, what a short walk it was, I sometimes wonder if she hoped Leonard might find the letter, come after her and save her.

We know she was wearing a fur coat and wellingtons for this last walk, and she had rocks in her pockets so that she didn't float. I've always liked that detail. It shows determination and planning, and I think suggests that she really didn't want to be saved.

Her body wasn't found until three weeks later, by which time the story of her disappearance was all over the newspapers, and Leonard even made a statement to the *New York Times*. He said that even in the absence of a body she had to be presumed dead. He didn't doubt her demise because he'd found her walking stick abandoned on the river bank, and she couldn't have walked without it.

15

Franklin Avenue is one of the less glamorous and less celebrated streets of Los Angeles. It runs parallel to, and north of, Sunset and Hollywood Boulevards but it lacks their fame and name recognition, and I'm sure a lot of local people think of it chiefly as an access road that gets them to the freeway. I used to live just off Franklin, and I can't say I was ever upset about this general lack of love for the street, because I knew that a walk along it always revealed a wonder or two.

There's the Shakespeare Bridge, there's the house where Gary Cooper lived with his parents, there's Sowdon House a few miles further along, a 'Mayan-revival' house built by Lloyd Wright, son of Frank. There's the 101 Coffee Shop, which in a previous incarnation featured in *Swingers*, a movie that plays cinematic havoc with the geography of east Hollywood and Los Feliz.

However, Vince Vaughn and Jon Favreau supposedly wrote the screenplay in the coffee shop, which you'd have thought would have led them to depict the area more or less faithfully.

Janis Joplin died of a heroin overdose in the Highland Gardens Hotel, at 7047 Franklin, a place I stayed when I first arrived in the city, along with my wife and her three cats, and the hotel is right next to the legendary Magic Castle, where magicians of varying degrees of finesse ply their trade.

But for me, and for others of a certain literary frame of mind, Franklin Avenue may be most notable as the street where Joan Didion and her husband John Gregory Dunne, lived in the late 1960s. Mentions of the 'Franklin Avenue house' crop up in various places in Didion's work, but most crucially in *The White Album*, published in 1979. She tells us that there was a former Canadian embassy on one side, a centre for Synanon (a dubious drug rehabilitation program) on the other. By her own account, things were extremely freewheeling inside her house.

She writes that a lot of people came and went through the house, and that she'd sometimes find people she didn't know sleeping in the beds. But things changed with the Manson killings and after that she and her husband and their daughter, Quintana Roo, moved away to a safer location. Didion said in an interview that a great many lives intersected with those of the Manson family. On the night of the Tate-LaBianca murders, they'd been driving along Franklin Avenue looking for victims. The kind of open house that Didion kept would have been ideal.

Although I regularly walked along various stretches of Franklin Avenue, only rarely did I go looking for the Didion house; it always seemed too difficult and too far away, at the other end of things, and I certainly didn't know the number. The only visual clues I had were in the famous Julian Wasser photographs of Joan and her yellow Corvette, though the photograph is black and white, in which all you can see is a section of wall and a perfectly ordinary looking garage. That didn't seem nearly enough to go on.

I had also seen a picture of Didion sitting on a balustrade, but I wasn't sure it was at the Franklin Avenue house, and in any case it was apparently in a back garden, and most likely wouldn't be visible from the street.

Finding the house wasn't a major obsession, and I can't say I actually craved to find the place, but then I was reading *The Year of Magical Thinking*, and found a reference to her going out to dinner at a house on Camino Palmero less than a block from where she used to live on Franklin. That was a revelation. If the

Didion-Dunnes had lived on Franklin Avenue, close by Camino Palmero, then surely it couldn't be too hard to find the place. I started walking.

As I approached what I knew had to be the right area, there were a surprising number of huge houses that looked like they might have been embassies at some time. Quite what a Synanon centre looked like, I had no idea. But I did notice quite a few big, new apartment buildings that had clearly been built since 1971, so it seemed possible that the Didion house might have been demolished in the intervening years. I did hope not.

Naturally, some walking quests are more prolonged than others, but to cut a short story even shorter, after a couple of the most minor false starts, I spotted the garage. There was no mistaking it. The two sliding doors seen in the Wasser photograph had been replaced by a single up and over, but the tiled roof, the molding below it, the size, and shape, were quite clearly the same. This was where Ms. D had parked her yellow Corvette, where she'd stood and posed for photographs. Eureka.

And what kind of house was attached to a garage like this? Well, rather a grand one it turned out, perhaps not strictly in the embassy class, but big and swanky enough for most tastes, and no doubt much refurbished since the Didion years. Zillow.com, I subsequently discovered, thought it was worth $3.3m.

The front garden gate was locked, though I wouldn't have gone in even if it had been open. I took seriously the 'armed response' threat that looms over so many houses in LA. However, there was a short, open driveway at the side of the house with parking for a few cars: only one was there now. By walking to the end of the driveway I'd be able to get a look into the back garden. I knew from reading my Didion that her daughter had played a lot of tennis on a court in there. Nobody was going to shoot me just for peering into the garden were they, surely?

And when I got to the end of the driveway, the side garden gate was wide open and there was a sign that read 'Welcome to Shumei Hollywood Garden'. It didn't exactly look public, but an open gate and a welcome sign says to me 'come on inside'. I'd never heard of Shumei: I figured it wasn't some Mansonite or even Synanon style organisation, though I guessed they were believers of some sort. In I went.

The garden was big, at least an acre, maybe two, and full of vegetable beds, in quantity, and elaborately arranged, with irrigation systems and trellises – it didn't look like it was just some hobbyist growing a few vegetables. There was no sign whatsoever of a tennis court. And there were no signs of any people either, nobody working in the garden, but I assumed there had to be somebody around somewhere because of the car on the drive. And, sure enough, after five minutes or so, a lean, delicate, serene young man came out of the house and offered greetings.

He gave me a very quick rundown on Shumei tenets: natural agriculture, art and beauty, spiritual enlightenment. Who's going to object to that? Shumei, I've since learned, also involves Jyorei 'a healing art that by focusing spiritual light gradually penetrates and dissolves the spiritual clouds that cause physical, emotional, and personal dilemmas.' The website has a first-person account of a woman who was cured of cancer. Yep, that old cookie. But the serene young man and I didn't go into that: actually, we had a discussion about gardening. The 'natural agriculture' they practice is staggeringly rigorous, no fertilizers allowed, not even the organic kind. I said how amazing it was to find this piece of lush horticultural land right here, so close to Hollywood Boulevard. Yes indeed, my young man agreed, and apparently it had once been very different, there'd even been a tennis court. I was ready to swoon.

The young man said he'd only been with Shumei for two years, and I may have been jumping to conclusions, but I didn't think he looked like a Didion reader, so I didn't turn the conversation that way, but he did tell me that the Shumei folks had been in residence for thirty-four years, which would mean they got there in 1979, some years after the Didion-Dunnes left, but in fact the same year that Didion's *The White Album* was published.

I didn't linger too long, not wanting to overstay my welcome, and to be honest I feared I might get roped in for some enforced spiritual enlightenment, but looking from the garden toward the house, I now saw a balustrade, unmistakably the very same one that Joan is sitting on in certain photographs. That pleased me so much. More than that, finding the house, finding this curious spiritual oasis, walking around the garden with this disciple, well, it all seemed very, very much like being inside a piece of writing by Joan Didion.

16

Even leaving aside the famous photographs with her Corvette, Didion never struck me as a woman who did a lot of walking – although when she wasn't in LA, she lived in New York for long periods of her life, and most people in New York are forced to be walkers one way or another. Her book *The Year of Magical Thinking* contains a few references to walking in the city in general and in Central Park in particular, and she mentions at one point that she stopped wearing sandals because they caught in the pavement, and she started wearing Puma sneakers instead. I tried without success to image what these Didion sandals actually looked like. I'd assumed she would be a wearer of sensible, flat ones, but if so, they surely wouldn't have caught in the pavement.

Then I read *Blue Nights* in which she says she had lived her whole life without thinking she'd ever get old, and that she'd imagined she'd always be able to wear her favourite red high-heeled sandals. This came as quite a surprise.

Did Joan Didion really walk the streets of Manhattan, or LA for that matter, wearing red suede sandals with high heels? If any pictures exist of her wearing these things, I have never seen them. Or is this further evidence that she didn't really do much walking at all? Was it all a writerly invention? It was Joan Didion who wrote, in *A Book of Common Prayer*, 'You have to pick the places you don't walk away from.'

17

I'm not a Charles Manson obsessive, but if you're of a certain age, if you've lived in or even visited Los Angeles, and if you also have a taste for walking in the desert, as I do, his name tends to come up once in a while. I've walked in parts of the Mojave Desert, where I was very definitely walking in the Manson family's footsteps. And I've been in the cab of Manson's wrecked old truck – a Dodge Power Wagon, which was still there in Ballarat when I last visited.

And then, despite not being a Manson obsessive, I did think I might try to visit the Barker Ranch, the last refuge of Manson and his family. I knew the place wasn't in great shape: a few years back a fire had destroyed all the wooden parts. I wondered if somebody had done this as an act of ritual cleansing but apparently not. The general wisdom is that somebody stayed there overnight, which hikers are completely entitled to do, and their propane stove got out of hand.

I also knew that to get to the Barker Ranch I'd have to drive up the Goler Wash. Online sources, as is the way, told me both that a moderately experienced driver of a 4 x 4 could zip up the Goler Wash without difficulty, while others said the route was a serious and potentially dangerous challenge. Conditions are no doubt changeable. The only question was whether I considered myself moderately experienced, and whether I was ready for a challenge.

Reyner Banham, the fine architectural critic and Anglo desert rat, said the greatest asset a person can have in the desert is 'creative cowardice,' and believing this, I drove to the mouth of Goler Canyon, parked, then walked up the wash to see if I thought I could handle driving up it.

Now, I'm not saying I couldn't have handled it. The canyon walls were narrow, the track was steep, there was water flowing down the wash (it had rained the previous night) and there were some rocky outcrops, described in the literature as steps or falls, places where a vehicle might get grounded or stuck, where you might pop a tyre or a wheel. I thought it was perfectly possible that my Jeep would pass over the obstacles, but it seemed perfectly possible that it wouldn't. Being stuck in Goler Wash, quite apart from the risks to self and vehicle, would have made me look like a complete idiot, something I generally try to avoid.

So I settled for a walk instead. It was a great walk. The canyon's walls were high but not oppressive. The rock was full of amazing colors. Cactuses grew up the slick sides, apparently sprouting straight out of the rock. There was also dung at the sides of the track, evidence that there were burros in the area, but I didn't see any of them.

I knew I wasn't going to walk all the way up to the Barker Ranch – it would have been a ten-mile round trip – and in any case it was just a burned-out cabin when you got there. Only later did I read that the fire at the Barker Ranch had given the Parks Service an interesting problem. They had contemplated restoring the place, not least to provide accommodation for hikers, but I think they feared they could be accused of restoring a Manson shrine, and maybe they also thought some anti-Mansonite would burn it down again, and so in the end they decided to leave it as it was, and it's now designated as an official 'ruin'.

18

Here's a good quiz question. What connects Scott Walker of the Walker Brothers with Charles Manson of the Manson family?

The first thing you may come up with is that the Walker brothers weren't really brothers, and that the Manson family wasn't really a family. That's true enough. You might also say that both Scott Walker and Charles Manson were using pseudonyms. Walker was originally Scott Engel, Manson was originally Charles Milles Maddox. But here's the real answer, which will get you bonus points: Charles Manson's biological father was called Walker Scott.

19

It seems to me, though I haven't seen any scientific data on the subject, that people who like walking tend also to like maps, though I'm not sure the reverse is true. Map lovers may well be content to gaze at charts and atlases and do their wandering mentally.

When I went abroad for the first time, on my own, in my late teens, to Nancy in France, to work on a dubious 'international youth project', one of the first things I did was buy a map of Nancy so that I could go walking, know where I was and where I was going.

'*Je voudrais une carte de Nancy*,' I said to the assistant in the local shop, and she understood what I was saying, which has pretty much been the high point of my French conversational career. The rest of the international youth on the project thought that buying a map was a very odd thing to do. I didn't try to explain it to them.

20

Later, when I first moved to London, not long after leaving university, of course I owned a London A-Z, as it seemed did everybody, more of a book than a map, and I carried it with me all the time: I wanted to know where I was, I wanted to know how to get where I was going and how to get home. This didn't strike me as odd either.

I was living in London because I'd got my first real job, working for a company named Bertram Rota that dealt in twentieth century literary first editions, as well as authors' manuscripts and the occasional item of literary memorabilia.

One of the company directors was George Lawson, a dapper, twinkly man of Scottish origins who was extremely well-connected, and never seemed to do anything that looked like work. He'd just stroll around the shop for most of the day, but at some point, he'd pick up the phone, call an important client, either an individual or a university library, and make a fabulous deal that earned the company, and him, a small fortune. I've always aspired to this way of working. He was friends with all manner of people in the art and literary worlds, including David Hockney, who was a regular visitor to the shop, and painted a rather wonderful portrait of George and his boyfriend of the time, the ballet dancer Wayne Sleep.

On one occasion George saw that I kept an A–Z in my bag. 'So,' he said, 'do you mean to say that when you go around London you take a MAP with you?' I said that I did. He found this both strange and hilarious. And my reaction at the time was, 'Doesn't everybody?' Surely, I thought, nobody knows the whole of London, and if you strayed anywhere outside your usual orbit you were going to need a map, weren't you? London is so vast and intricate, with so many obscure corners, how could you get around without one?

I didn't say that to George, and in retrospect I'm glad that I didn't, and of course once I'd lived in London for a while I didn't carry an A–Z with me all the time. And that's surely how it always is once you know something of a city. I didn't know every street, didn't have a complete mental map of London imprinted in my head, but

I'd developed a feel for the place, had a general sense of direction, a sense of how neighborhoods related to each other. This was based on the experience of walking, of knowing the city on the ground, not on a map, and of course there were occasions when I went to some completely unknown part of the city, in which case I dug out my A–Z again.

21

Dennis Wood, author of *The Power of Maps* and *Everything Sings: Maps for A Narrative Atlas* was interviewed by *The Believer* magazine. He talked about the idea that street signs and names are only for strangers: when a place is part of you, you don't need a street sign telling you where you are. He obviously has a point. Later he describes the experience of arriving in a city, checking into a hotel, then wandering the streets for a couple of hours. He says you don't notice the street names, you just remember turning left or right, or a landmark.

This is true too, and a familiar enough experience, but there's a contradiction here, isn't there? If the above is true, then the street names *aren't* for strangers: or at least the stranger in this case isn't paying any attention to them.

It also raises the question of how far away from home you have to be before you're considered a stranger.

Unless you always stay within an incredibly limited number of streets then sooner or later you'll find a street sign extremely useful.

Actually, I also wonder just how many people spend two hours walking the streets around their hotel these days. I do, of course, and I know I'm not the only one, but I suspect a lot of the people who arrive in a new city and want to get some exercise are more likely to head for the safety of the hotel gym, pool or spa, rather than walking the streets. They don't know what they're missing. Or maybe they do.

22

Meanwhile, back at Bertram Rota, there was an occasion when we were selling some Somerset Maugham
memorabilia, including a walking stick. I imagine it
may have been one of many, but it was an impressive
thing, made of very dark wood, and embossed with the
famous Maugham 'hand of Fatima' symbol to ward off
the evil eye.

George Lawson spent most of one day pretending
to be lame, hobbling up and down the shop, using
Maugham's walking stick for support. He was very con-
vincing, and customers who knew him showed great
concern and sympathy, and asked how he'd come to
injure himself. He found this even more hilarious.

23

Hockney was a regular visitor to the shop, and we kept a large pile of his *David Hockney on David Hockney* on a table that confronted you as you walked in the door. That was Hockney's autobiographical book from the 1970s, now subtitled 'My Early Years.' Back then at least, he was the kind of man who liked to wander the streets around his hotel, in one case in Santa Monica California, which he describes in the book.

He writes about checking into a motel and then walking on the beach. He was looking for the town, but he couldn't see it. Then he saw some lights and thought that must be the centre of things, so he walked a couple of miles and at the end of the walk he discovered that the light belonged to a large gas station on the edge of town. So he walked back again.

I think that if he'd had a map he'd have known better.

24

In 2000 I published a novel titled *Bleeding London*: it remains one of my greatest hits. Among many other things it contains a character named Stuart London who sets out to walk down every street in London. Yes, names are destiny. He carries an A–Z with him, blacking out the streets once he's walked them, so he ends up with a completely obliterated (and essentially useless) map. I like to think that the current state of mapping either on your phone or by printing off pages from Google maps, makes this notion more rather than less poignant.

The book was considered a success (these things are always comparative). A couple of years later *Time Out* ran a piece titled 'London's Most Erotic Writers' and I came in nineteenth, on the basis of *Bleeding London*, which I thought wasn't bad, considering that Walter, author of *My Secret Life* came in number one, and

Shakespeare came in number seven. And I was chuffed to find I was ten places ahead of my old hero JG Ballard.

I think I owed my place on that list to Deborah Moggach who I used to know slightly, though not well enough for this to count as nepotism. She lists one of her recreations as 'walking around London looking into people's windows.' Well, yes. Who doesn't do that given half a chance? But how many, apart from Deborah, admit it in print?

Deborah and I definitely walked some short distances on the streets of London together, but we never found anybody's window to look into, which I think we would both consider a shame.

25

Over the years various people have wanted to 'do something' with my novel, turn it into a movie, TV series or comic book. I've always said, 'Great, go ahead,' but nothing has ever come of it; it has steadfastly remained a book. So when I got an email from somebody named Del Barrett of the Royal Photographic Society saying she wanted to curate a photographic exhibition based on *Bleeding London*, I again said sure, go for it, but never really expected to hear from her again.

Oh me of little faith. Not so very much later I was there in a pop-up gallery in Pimlico for the official launch of 'Bleeding London: the Exhibition,' which according to the press release was 'the most ambitious photo project that the capital has ever seen – to photograph every street in London. Based on the Whitbread shortlisted novel, *Bleeding London* by Geoff Nicholson, we are challenging Londoners and visitors to follow in the footsteps of Stuart London and cover the entire A-Z.'

The standard A-Z at that time had 73,000 entries, though only about 58,000 of those were streets. That was a number that sometimes made the project seem utterly insane. At other times however, I thought oh well, let's imagine the RPS can round up 1,000 committed photographers, that's only fifty-eight streets each, and these guys can take a couple of hundred pictures in a day, so that seems perfectly doable.

Wanting to be involved, and determined to show I was willing, while I was in London, I walked all the streets in a single square of the A-Z as determined by Del Barrett, covering part of Lewisham. And frankly it was absolutely knackering, mentally as much as physically (although the expedition only took a little more than three hours), as I walked up Algernon Street and tramped along Marsala Street and flogged along Shell Street and meandered the length of Vicar's Hill (among many others) and finally ended up in Loampit Vale, taking photographs as I went.

Back in those days I sometimes, but by no means always, carried a camera with me when I went walking, but if I took half a dozen photographs in the course of an afternoon I thought that was plenty. How things change. Like everybody else I now have a camera of one kind or another with me pretty much all of the time, and like everybody else I take far too many pictures.

The interesting thing about the Bleeding London photo project was that it created the impetus, the necessity, of finding something to photograph in every single street. You could argue that there was something very democratic about this process, maybe something very Zen. As you walk, every street becomes equal, you have to find something of interest, something 'worth' observing and photographing regardless of where you are and regardless of what the streets are like.

It wasn't always easy. On my afternoon of photography certain streets seemed to offer multiple attractions, some seemed a bit dull, and offered nothing whatsoever at first glance. The job therefore was to look harder, to see through the perceived dullness and find the things that are worthy of attention. And although the majority of the streets were suburban and very quiet (I like suburban streets very much), there were some oddities, the detached sidecar from a motorbike that looked like a rocket ship from an old fairground ride, a Zombie Outbreak Response Vehicle, among them.

Inevitably not every picture I took was massively interesting, and there was a certain reliance on my own set of clichés: show me a corrugated metal fence or a semi-derelict garage and I'll snap away with intensity. And sometimes – and this was a curious and unexpected thing, and relevant to Dennis Wood's proposition, the street signs themselves were as fascinating and picturesque as anything in the street.

All in all, it was a strange mission, involving a curious sort of discipline. It was definitely a walk with a purpose, but by no means a walk from A to B (let alone from A to Z). It represented a way of exploring the territory, making it (in a very limited sense) my own, exhausting it even as I exhausted myself. There's quite a lot about this kind of thing in the novel.

I kept thinking I was involved with a sort of minimalist or conceptualist art project, something Sol LeWitt would have approved of. I don't claim that Sol LeWitt is a completely open book to me, but I do know that he said, 'When an artist uses a conceptual form of art, it means that all of the planning and decisions are made beforehand, and the execution is a perfunctory affair. The idea becomes a machine that makes the art.' Who wouldn't want that?

26

In due course, there was a *Bleeding London* exhibition at London's City Hall, of photographs inspired by my novel. Amazingly, improbably, they'd succeeded – 58,000 streets, 58,000 photographs and a preliminary display of 1,200 images was shown in the exhibition. The further plan was that at some point there'd be a gigantic exhibition of all the photographs in a vast warehouse somewhere in London, and there'd be an online archive as well, but you know, the best laid plans …

To tie in with the exhibition, there was a walk conducted by Jen Pedler, who's a walking guide as well as a photographer, and was formerly a Volkswagen mechanic, titled 'Stuart's First Walk' – a nice five-mile meander based on a description in the book of my character's first foray into tramping all the streets of London. He (and I) chose North Pole Road, in W10, as the starting point, largely because of the name.

'He knew he had to begin somewhere and he knew that in one sense, any place was as good as another, but he scanned the index of his A–Z looking for a street name that sounded appropriate. His eyes fell on a line that read North Pole Road. Next day he went there and started his walk.'

In the beginning Stuart just walks for the sake of it, but then he starts keeping a diary because he realises he's forgetting what he's seen, and I do know the feeling, although as I proved, writing things down is no absolute guarantee that you'll remember them. Photographs surely stick in the mind a bit better. In my own occasional wearying attempts to turn Bleeding London into a screenplay I've always said to producers that in a movie version Stuart should be keeping a photo or video diary rather than a written one; but that has always been the least of the problems.

And so we guided walkers went with Jen Pedler along North Pole Road, following in Stuart London's, and to some extent my, old footsteps. Full, unsurprising, disclosure: I by no means walked every street in London while writing the book. This is the joy of writing fiction – you can make stuff up, though of course we all know that writers of non-fiction make stuff up too. But there were some days when I pretended to be Stuart, walked where he walked, and certainly the book contains descriptions of things I actually saw while walking in London, not least in North Pole Road.

Having the author himself on a walking tour based on his book was a curious thing, not least for the author. Someone had said to Jen that it would be like walking with Dickens, and yeah, sure that's *exactly* what it was like. Jen had considered having me read out various passages as we walked, but in the event she decided against it, for which I was truly grateful. It would have been excruciating for all concerned, but especially excruciating for me.

The walk took place a good eighteen years after the book was published, and I'm not a great re-reader of my own work, so I was pretty vague about some of the things I'd seen and described in the novel. Other things, of course seemed clear as day. Things in North Pole Road, however, fell chiefly into the former category: without the book I'd have remembered hardly anything at all.

The pub that had once been called the North Pole and then the New North Pole had been converted into a Tesco Express after much local protest, apparently. But there was still a florist and hairdresser as mentioned in the book, and there was still Mick's Fish Bar and also the newsagent which in the book I called Varishna's which I then learned was a misspelling.

And we walked beyond North Pole Road, seeing some things I remembered and rather more things I'd forgotten. We walked by Wormwood Scrubs – the prison and the piece of land with the same name. We went up Scrubs Lane, along part of the Harrow Road, across the Grand Union Canal and eventually past Ernö Goldfinger's Trellick Tower, and then to Ladbroke Grove.

I think the most satisfying moment came on the Harrow Road. There's a moment in the book when Stuart sees 'a tyre centre whose frontage had a mural depicting members of staff.' I'd completely forgotten about this, and when Jen Pedler had done a reccie of the route, she hadn't been able to find it either, and yet suddenly there it was, and all we Bleeding Londoners stood outside, staring in quiet wonder, celebrating, taking photographs, while the guys who worked there, the current employees who were not depicted on the mural, looked out at us with suspicion.

I find it's always hard work to walk in a group, any group. The good thing about being with a bunch of photographers is that you can wander off by yourself and look at little curiosities and take pictures and everybody else understands. It slows the walk down, but it also sharpens your perceptions as you try to find new things to photograph, avoiding the more obvious stuff that everybody else is photographing.

27

When *Bleeding London* was first published, I was invited to do a reading at a bookshop in Charing Cross Road, along with the mighty Iain Sinclair who was promoting his breakthrough book *Lights Out for the Territory: 9 Excursions in the Secret History of London*.

One of my prized possessions from that event is a copy of the book that Sinclair signed for me. The inscription reads, 'For Geoff – black this out as you go along. With best wishes, Iain.' Very cool, and needless to say I haven't done that.

One of the many great things he writes in the book, 'The faster we walk, the more ground we lose.'

28

I'm not sure I was ever really part of the big London-centric, psychogeographic, drifting, topographic, historic, highbrow, hairy-chested, fiction and non-fiction thing. This was at least partly because I moved to New York shortly after my book was published, but it was a real enough phenomenon at the time, exemplified by Sinclair, Will Self, Patrick Keiller, Peter Ackroyd, and a meteor shower of other writers.

Some of it seems pretty well played out now, although I recently read Will Wiles' 2019 novel *Plume* which is smart enough to acknowledge the attractions of psycho-geography while also making mock of it. Wiles puts the chief objections into the mouth of a fictional writer, one Oliver Pierce, who's complaining about his career and says 'I was lumped in with all that psychogeography lot … There are so many people doing that shit now. All the fucking lost rivers, ghost Tube stations, all that shit … It makes me want to puke. It was getting boring ten years ago, it's just intolerable now.'

It's hard to tell from the novel whether Wiles completely agrees with his creation, but really, what's to argue about? In the end, he does concede semi-positively that walking, thought and writing all go together, but he adds: 'In London, the dérive has come adrift. A form of writing that I once aspired to has expired.'

Is the psychogeographical party really over? I suspect so, and it wasn't a party I was ever really invited to, and yet like many parties it kind of drags on.

29

I'm sure it must be possible to walk the streets of Vienna without whistling or singing to yourself 'The Blue Danube,' but for a first-time visitor like me, it wasn't easy: Air Austria even played it over the aircraft's p.a. system as we were deplaning. Other alternative mental soundtracks include the *Third Man* theme, or the well-known Ultravox tune – and although the latter does have some oblique lyrics that mention walking, the only line anybody ever remembers is the one about Vienna meaning nothing to me, which seemed a bit negative and insulting for a new arrival to sing about a city.

I was in Vienna for the launch of a photographic project called Wiener Blut, also organised by Del Barrett, 'an ambitious collaboration to photograph every street in Vienna. As well as creating a work of art for an exhibition in 2018, we'll be producing a visual social documentary of Vienna in 2017/18.' It was to be a European cousin of Bleeding London. Alas, it never happened.

At the Vienna launch I made a short, clumsy speech in English about walking and observing and photographing. The usual stuff: I said that every street is interesting if you look at it the right way. There are fascinations, marvels, on every block, probably on every square inch, and I still profoundly believe this to be true.

After, and even before, that launch I wandered the streets of Vienna, sometimes alone, sometimes with others, looking at things, taking pictures, feeling the vibe, sometimes getting lost. Walking down the street from my hotel, I came across a place named f*c, which I think stood for Frauencafe, a women's café. There was a mission statement in the window, in both German and English. The English one read that if you were a cis-gendered man, you should leave the space without having to be asked. This seemed to anticipate an unlikely set of events; that a cis-gendered man (I guess that would me) might walk into the place, by accident, or perhaps to see how great it was, or in any case without having read the sign in the window, but then he would immediately have to walk out again before he was asked to do so, but how would he know to do that unless he'd read the sign in the window? And if he'd read the sign in the window then surely he wouldn't enter, would he? And what would happen if he *did* wait to be asked? Who would ask? Surely they'd *tell*. In any case the place was always closed every time I walked past.

30

Like any good tourist, I gazed into shop windows as I walked around the city. I swear I saw a shop that sold only booze and light bulbs. You can imagine the thought process: people are always going to need booze, people are always going to need light bulbs – there's your business model.

And then there was a walk around the Flak Towers of Vienna – I hadn't known about them, and I definitely should have. They're giant concrete, fortress-like structures, some forty meters high. There are similar towers in Berlin and Hamburg, and although I've walked in both those cities, I never saw the Flak Towers.

Building of the Vienna models started in 1942 on Hitler's instructions. They were constructed using forced labour, naturally, and they were functional by 1944, which might be thought to be a bit late. There were guns at the top on the outside, and an air raid shelter inside, and lord knows they were solid and impregnable. They're still wildly impressive in their totalitarian brutality.

Jan Tabor, the Czech-Austrian architect and architectural theorist said they were

mood architecture, signifiers of an idea about power, stability and the will to live. They are monuments of and for all times. As a result, they are without utilitarian value in the usual sense. They are as useless as plastic art. But they were carriers of an idea, an elementary feeling for power, stability and will to live.

As I walked around them, in what is now a very pleasant public park, it seemed that the local walkers failed to appreciate the mood and ignored the towers completely. Maybe they were too familiar with them, or maybe they hated them and preferred not to look, or even acknowledge their existence while walking. That may have been the best way to treat them.

31

And speaking of Viennese blood, if not blood and soil, I did see a graffito '*Jesus pisst dein Blut*', which I believe translates as 'Jesus pisses your blood.' How he'd get your, or my, blood, into his bladder I'm not sure. It made me think of the Vienna Actionists, a well-dodgy bunch of 1960s artists, performance artists as we'd call them today, whose 'actions' tended to involve blood, excreta, cruelty to animals, blasphemy and sex (most of the sex very unerotic, I'd say, but these things are subjective).

It was all about breaking taboos and making Austrians face up to their country's embrace of Nazism in the Second World War, apparently. I think you're entitled to wonder how rolling around in animal entrails symbolises these matters, but it was a different age.

Still, if you inevitably walk in Vienna in the foot-steps of Strauss and Thomas Bernhard, Graham Greene and Sigmund Freud, you also walk in the footsteps of Günter Brus, Hermann Nitsch, Rudolf Schwarzkogler and Otto Muehl, the four main Actionists. Muehl was the best known and most spectacularly appalling of them, and he was also the leader of a radical commune, as was the style at the time, and a thing that seldom ends well.

In 1968, Günter Brus went to jail as a result of 'Body Analysis Action no.33,' which involved cutting himself with a razor blade, drinking his own urine, rubbing his naked body with feces and masturbating while singing the Austrian anthem. He got six months for 'degrading the symbols of the State.' Personally, I think people should be allowed to degrade the symbols of the state, but given Austrian law, I can't believe Brus was very surprised to be jailed. Perhaps he wanted to be.

Before that however, in 1965, he performed 'Vienna Walk' (Kopfbemalung, Aktion, Wien) a fairly vanilla-seeming piece in which he walked through the city, fully clothed but painted all white, with a black line that, at least in photographs, looks like medical stitches, dividing his body (and indeed his suit) into two vertical halves, claiming himself to be a 'living painting'. Sounds pretty harmless, but he still got arrested.

Otto Muehl in due course went to jail on charges of having sex with underage girls at his commune. No big surprise there. Günter Brus was awarded the Grand Austrian State Prize in 1997. Maybe the Austrian State is a walking mass of contradictions.

32

Sometimes you watch a movie (not anything by the Vienna Actionists, obviously) and you think, 'This movie has been made with precisely me in mind.' The corollary may be that sometimes you think you might be the only person on earth who actually wants to see the said movie. In the case of Gus Van Sant's *Gerry* (2002) this isn't literally true: the Internet reveals a few diehard fans, but there are a great many more who hate it with a hard and gemlike flame.

If IMDb is to be believed, the movie cost $3.5 million to make and brought in $26,000 on its opening weekend, which will surely come as no surprise to anybody who's seen it: this is not a movie destined to pack them into the multiplexes. The most amazing thing may be that the movie ever got made at all. According to some sources, people 'walked out in droves' at early screenings. I don't believe I've ever walked in a drove.

The 'action' consists almost entirely of walking in the desert (actually several deserts), and the plot is very straightforward. Two guys – Matt Damon and Casey Affleck, who refer to each other as Gerry though that may well not be their 'real' names – go for a walk in the desert, going down a 'wilderness trail' in order to see 'the thing' that it leads to. (We never learn what the 'thing' is.) They get lost and try to find their way back – and that's pretty much it for the next ninety minutes or so.

There's a lot of walking and not much talking. The guys have no food or water with them, and they don't find any, and although it's not clear how long they're actually lost, you can't help thinking they'd be dead, or at least incapacitated, very soon indeed, in which case there'd be no movie. But maybe that's an over-literal response. Perhaps this desert walk is metaphysical rather than geographical. One wag on Rotten Tomatoes describes it as 'Hiking with Godot'. I wish I'd said that.

The two guys walk in one or two desert places that were recognisable to me – Death Valley and the salt flats of Utah. However, and I only worked this out afterwards from the credits, they actually set out in Argentina, which was where they started shooting the movie, but Van Sant was dissatisfied with the results. Certainly, the desert in the early part of the movie is much less picturesque than that in the States.

The movie is probably genuinely and intentionally 'boring', though I've certainly been more bored by movies in which much more happened. However, since the two stars are Hollywood actors, I kept fearing that they, or Van Sant, or somebody, would lose their nerve and the movie would go all 'Hollywood' at the end with fist fights and car chases, maybe a gratuitous sex scene. But that doesn't happen. Everybody keeps their nerve; more or less. It's a truly great walking movie, and there aren't many of those.

33

Another surprising thing about *Gerry* is that the movie was 'based on a true story', that of David Coughlin and Raffi Kodikian, two hikers who in 1999 got lost (rather less symbolically, though no less existentially) in Rattlesnake Canyon, part of the Carlsbad Caverns National Park in New Mexico.

Kodikian and Coughlin were actually better equipped than the Gerries of the Van Sant movie. They had three pints of water and a pint of Gatorade, and they did have a map, though it seems they didn't know how to use it. And they got far more desperate than the Gerries; licking rocks, eating cactus fruit, drinking their own urine. Anyway it all ended very badly in a 'mercy killing'. After three days Coughlin was dehydrated and vomiting and begged Kodikian to kill him, which he did.

According to Kodikian's journal, 'I killed & burried (sic) my best friend today. Dave had been in pain all night. At around 5 or 6, he turned to me and begged that I put my knife through his chest. I did, and a second time when he wouldn't die.' The general opinion of the autopsy reports is that this was very premature. Both guys were dehydrated, but survivably so, as Kodikian demonstrated.

Kodikian was found guilty of second-degree murder, sentenced to fifteen years, all but two of them suspended, and in the end he served only sixteen months. This isn't what happens in *Gerry*.

Having been quite lost (briefly, mercifully) a couple of times in the desert, I'm not at all smug about these matters, and I'm well aware how quickly a casual walk can turn into a nightmare, but the word online is that Rattlesnake Canyon is an amazingly benign piece of territory, an easy trail with water and toilets nearby. Interestingly, nobody seems to mention the presence of rattlesnakes.

Of course, this apparently benign quality is often part of the problem, and I'm not being metaphysical here. I simply mean that when you know you're walking somewhere dangerous, you tend to be on your mettle, to be careful, you tend not to take chances. It's when you feel safe that you can get into real trouble.

34

Which gets us back to Death Valley and four German tourists who died there in the summer of 1996. There always seem to be lot of Germans driving around the American deserts, but few of them do it with such reckless abandon as Cornelia Meyer and Egbert Rimkus, who were with their two children. They were on vacation in the States; they rented a minivan in Los Angeles and headed for Death Valley. They disappeared in late July, in a week when temperatures reached over 49 degrees.

In October that year their van was found in sand in a ravine off Anvil Spring Canyon, probably not a route to tackle in a minivan. All four tires were wrecked: the van was locked and abandoned. Clothes, sleeping bags, rolls of exposed film and a couple of beers, had been left in the vehicle, but the tourists had taken their personal belongings – such as passports, wallets and air tickets – with them. They had evidently made the decision to walk out of there. There were no tracks showing which way they'd gone, although a beer bottle, similar to the ones in the car, was found half a mile away. A major search operation began that included the use of horses and helicopters. But all involved would have known they were months too late, and in the event they found nothing.

And indeed nothing at all was found for the next thirteen years until late 2009 when a couple of hikers, actually two members of the Riverside Mountain Rescue team, found skeletal remains and identification, just a few miles from the abandoned van, which only goes to prove that a full-scale desert search is not guaranteed to find, much less save, you. Reports said the remains were found southeast of Goler Wash, which, as discussed earlier leads to the Barker Ranch where Manson and certain members of his 'family' were captured.

When I tell people that I like walking in the desert, even alone, they sometimes ask, 'Isn't it scary? Aren't you afraid you're going to encounter some Charles Manson type?' The answer is no, I'm really not scared of that. And the truth is, you're as likely to meet some Charles Manson type on Hollywood Boulevard, or even on

Oxford Street, as you are in Death Valley. Out there in the desert, you have far more to fear from yourself and your own failings.

35

I was in the gas station in Stove Pipe Wells, in Death Valley, filling up my car, prior to driving off into the wilds to do some walking, when a big but unthreatening man standing nearby said to me, 'So how do you like my desert?'

The gas station was also a general store and I think he worked there, though I couldn't be sure.

I said I liked the desert very much, and I didn't argue about whether or not it was his.

He could tell that I was a city dweller because he then said, 'If you walk on concrete for too long you start to think like a predator 'cause everybody wants something from you.'

There was no answer to that, but I nodded, finished putting gas in the car and drove on. A couple of minutes later I pulled the car over and wrote down what the man had said, a thing I very rarely do.

I wrote it on the back of a free postcard I'd picked up at Pappy and Harriet's bar in Pioneertown. The card went into the mass of disorganised files that constitute my 'archive'. It stayed there 'lost' for fifteen years before I came across it again while I was writing this book.

There's no doubt that I've done a lot of walking on concrete, but as far as I know, I don't think like a predator.

36

Fernando Pessoa says, on the subject of walking, writing and forgetfulness, 'While out walking I've formulated perfect phrases which I can't remember when I get home. I'm not sure if the ineffable poetry of these phrases belongs totally to what they were and which I forget, or partly to what they after all weren't.'

No use suggesting he could have got himself a Moleskine, though admittedly that might not have solved all his problems.

Some time ago, I was digging around in an old notebook of mine, looking for something else, and I happened to find this, scrawled in my own handwriting. It appeared to be a quotation:

He was walking in America, always heading west, dodging cars, walking with ghosts and madmen, with saints and scream queens and with those who refused to ride the bus: Thoreau and Kerouac. Sometimes it was a lonely walk.

I have no idea where I got this or who it's a quotation from, if anyone — Don DeLillo? Steve Erickson? Jim Harrison? — and although I've searched from time to time to find its source, I'm still no wiser. I'm as sure as I can be that I didn't write it myself, but you can never be absolutely sure about these things; literary amnesia is a condition most writers have to live with.

On the other hand, if you go online and search for 'Geoff Nicholson quotations' you'll find a quotation attributed to me about walking on a suburban street at night, each house with its own little blue square of a television shining out through uncurtained windows.

Now that one I'm absolutely sure I didn't write, because I know who did. It was Jack Kerouac, and it's from *The Dharma Bums*.

I used to be absolutely obsessed with Kerouac's work, and partly with the man himself. I wrote a dissertation on his work at university, and I did a lot of hitchhiking and bus riding around the United States believing I was following in his footsteps. I don't have the same passion for Kerouac's writing that I once did, and sometimes I think I've outgrown him, but any time I go back and reread his work, I'm reminded why it moved me so much in the first place: the openness, the vulnerability, the sense that the world is a place full of possibilities.

There's another passage in *The Dharma Bums* in which Kerouac advises the walker to just look at the trail at your feet, until you fall into a kind of walking trance. 'Trails are like that: you're floating along in a Shakespearean Arden paradise and expect to see nymphs and fluteboys, then suddenly you're struggling in a hot broiling sun of hell in dust and nettles and poison oak... just like life.'

That's great, isn't it? And fluteboys! Who'd ever have associated Kerouac with fluteboys?

37

I was walking in downtown Los Angeles, a place where (despite the bad press that LA gets as a pedestrian hell) a lot of others walk too. It was a busy weekday lunchtime and the streets were full of people. There was a lot to look at, a lot of distractions, and that was why I wasn't paying much attention to the youngish, hippyish man who was standing not very far away from me as we both waited for the light to change so we could cross the street.

It turned out he was a panhandler, however, and apparently he'd been trying and failing to get my attention for a while, and he thought I was deliberately ignoring him, which was unfair and untrue. I hadn't been sufficiently aware of him to deliberately ignore him, though if I had been, I might have done. And now he said loudly, pointedly, in a sneering tone that did finally get my attention, 'Hey, who do you think you are? Jack Kerouac?'

Yes, he really said that, and I have no idea what he meant by it. My physical resemblance to Jack Kerouac is non-existent, and in any case Kerouac was surely not the kind of man who went around ignoring panhandlers or bums of any kind. He usually embraced them in a Zen kind of way. Still, as sneering insults go, this wasn't the worst, and I actually found it funny. I still didn't respond to the panhandler: what would I have said? But then the light changed and I walked across the street with a big smile on my face. That probably only made things worse for the guy.

38

Jack Kerouac died long before I was in any position to meet him, in fact before I'd even heard of him. I'm sure I could have met Lawrence Ferlinghetti in the City Lights Bookshop in San Francisco, but I missed my chance. I did however once meet Beat poet Gary Snyder, 'meet' as in go backstage after he'd read at the LA Book Festival, shake his hand and say, 'I really enjoyed your reading.'

I wasn't lying when I said that. I think he's probably the best poetry reader I've ever seen and heard. And I don't think I'm just being sentimental towards the old guy. Beforehand, I did wonder what shape he'd be in; to which the answer was, 'Probably better shape than you and me.'

Snyder makes an appearance in Iain Sinclair's book *American Smoke*. Sinclair goes to visit him at his hundred-acre estate in the Sierra foothills, north of Nevada

City, California (Allen Ginsberg and Dick Baker were co-owners at one time, but he bought them out). Sinclair describes Snyder as a poet, bioregionalist, teacher, skier, climber and trail walker. Sinclair is also a little scathing about the way Snyder treated his wives, making lists of their faults for instance. I didn't bring that up when I met Snyder, but meeting with Sinclair and the book did get mentioned.

'Oh yeah,' said Snyder, 'that was a funny piece.'

I still don't know if he meant funny ha ha, or funny peculiar.

In the course of the reading, Snyder quoted from Basho's text, generally known as *The Narrow Road to the Deep North*, though he referred to it as *The Narrow Trails to the Back Country*, which sounds like a very different proposition.

One line in the text runs, 'How true it is that if men strive to walk in the way of truth and uphold righteousness, fame will follow of itself.'

I suspect this is one of the least true things Basho or anyone else has ever said.

39

Obviously the youngish, hippyish man who accosted me in downtown LA didn't actually think I was Jack Kerouac, who'd been dead for at least forty-five years at the time. And the man who once stopped me as I was walking down the street in Hudson, New York and said, 'Do you know you look just like Dave Stewart of Eurythmics?' he didn't really think I was Dave Stewart. And I, of course, didn't think I looked at all like Dave Stewart, but I could have been wrong.

However, LA being what it was and is, the man who stopped me while I was walking in Griffith Park and said, 'Hey, you're that guy from *Die Hard*, aren't you?' I believe he really might have thought I was the guy (or anyway, a guy) from the film. In fact, I'm not sure he really believed me when I said I wasn't.

I went home and searched IMDb to see which of

the many guys in the film I could possibly resemble. Not Bruce Willis, obviously, and surely not Alan Rickman though he and I did both have beards at the time, and going down the cast list of Various African-Americans, members of other minorities e.g. Al Leong, James Shigeta and Alexander Gudonov, and a bunch of actors I'd never heard of but definitely didn't look like, I concluded that the guy in the park was just one of those vaguely delirious guys you often find walking around in parks.

However my best 'recognition' came when I was, unexpectedly and unwillingly, walking around the parking lot of the LA zoo. My car had overheated while I was on the freeway, and this was the nearest place to pull in. I was waiting for a tow truck to arrive, and it was obviously going to be a while, so I was walking around as a form of displacement activity. Then a police cruiser pulled up and the driver asked me what I was up to. He was a real cop, though I imagine the Zoo Beat is not where they put their brightest and best, and he was friendly enough.

I explained my problem, pointed to the steaming, broken down car, and he accepted that as a perfectly good explanation. Then right before he drove off he looked me over and said, 'Hey, do I know you? You've got a really familiar face. Have I seen you in the movies?'

I said that was not possible, and he accepted this too, though he couldn't quite get over the fact that I looked familiar, and as a parting shot he said, 'Oh well, maybe I arrested you sometime.'

See, not all LA cops are monsters, at least not if you're white, middle-aged, more or less middle-class, unarmed and with a plausible story.

40

When people used to ask me why I'd moved to Los Angeles I always said, 'Oh, I came for the walking.' That was met with varying degrees of hilarity. Then I said it was actually for the wild flora and fauna, the amazing architecture and the cool old cars. This was almost true. But even in the time I lived there, about fifteen years, the number of cool old cars reduced a lot.

There's supposed to be some fundamental conflict between driving and walking, between drivers and walkers, but it's a false opposition if you ask me. I enjoy both driving and walking. When I'm walking, I try not to hate drivers. When I'm driving, I try not to hate walkers. Sometimes it takes a bit of effort, but on the whole I manage to stay tolerant.

The fact is I do like cars very much, the stranger and cooler and more patinated, the better. I've owned and lived with a few 'interesting' cars, but I've concluded that the more interesting a car is, the more trouble it's likely to be. I still like cool old cars, I just don't have any desire to own one. Owning cool old cars has resulted in me doing a fair amount of unplanned and unwanted walking when they die in the middle of a trip, in a car park, on a motorway, in the middle of nowhere. These days I prefer to look.

And when I'm out walking and I see a classic vehicle, then I go across the street and have a good look, and in some circumstances I take a picture. As vicarious pleasures go, I think it's harmless enough, although I do seem to recall reading Kingsley Amis's opinion that crossing the street to look at a car was the very definition of being a bore. It does not surprise me that Amis senior would find me boring, for all kinds of reasons.

I have also abandoned a principle that I employed when I first lived in Los Angeles. My wife and I owned one car and she used it every day to go to work, so obviously I needed a car of my own. It didn't need to be a great car or even a very good car, because if I had some serious driving to do I could always use the other one, but I did need a car of my own.

I couldn't face going to a used car dealer so I came up with a scheme: I would walk the streets of Los Angeles and sooner or later I'd come across a car with a 'for sale' sign in the window and that would be MY car, the car I was destined to own. That's how I ended up with a 1966 powder blue, slant six, Dodge Dart. It was a good car, in many ways a great car, and it served me very well indeed for the first thirteen of the fifteen years I owned it. In the world of old cars that seemed a pretty good result.

41

I never understand people who need music while walking, who even compile playlists to listen to as they walk. For that matter I never understand those, Baudrillard among them, who talk about the silence of the desert. Deserts are rarely if ever silent. There's wind, there are birds, and over large parts of the American desert there are likely to be jet fighters. I like to be able to hear the noises going on around me, whatever they may be. Which inevitably brings us to John Cage.

It's hard, for some of us anyway, to think about silence without thinking about Cage. It's also hard to think of Cage as a son of the Los Angeles suburbs, but that's where he grew up, in a comparatively modest Arts and Crafts style bungalow.

The house was, and still is, at 2708 Moss Avenue in Eagle Rock, a neighbourhood in northeast LA, ethnically diverse but currently with some serious hipster elements, and gentrifying all the time. When I was in LA I took a walk to see the house. I went with my LA walking pal Anthony Miller.

We drove over to Eagle Rock and parked far enough away from Moss Avenue that it would feel like an expedition or at least a good walk. It was a typical Los Angeles day in late May, sunny, hot and getting hotter, but bearable at least for a couple of hours. Eagle Rock looked very suburban in that Los Angeles way: low-rise, single-family houses, modest architecture, though no two houses were exactly alike, often with diverse cacti, succulents and palm trees growing in the front yards.

Moss Avenue runs southeast to northwest, from Eagle Rock Boulevard, up to the 2 Freeway, though that freeway wouldn't have been there in Cage's time. A sound-reducing wall helps keep in the roar of traffic on the freeway, though it by no means creates silence. Cage would have a lot to say.

The house was built from scratch by Cage's own father (also named John). Cage senior was an inventor by profession, who worked on early versions of colour television, sonar, and a 'Mist-A-Cold' medical inhaler. His most famous project was a failed diesel submarine.

There was a lot of boom and bust in the Cage family, moments of considerable wealth and success, other times when the furniture had to be sold to make ends meet. I suppose the good thing about having that kind of father is that there's no pressure on a son to settle down and get a steady job, although both Cage parents were well-connected enough to ensure that their son took music lessons and had some interesting extracurricular teachers.

It's perhaps no surprise that a man who can build his own submarine can also build his own home, though it's perhaps more surprising that Cage senior should have built such a conventional-looking suburban ranch house as the one on Moss Avenue. It was a house much like any other in the street. The garden path was set off-centre, to the right as you're looking at the house, and it led to five short steps that would take you up to an open porch and the front door. There were pillars either side of the steps with circular topped niches. These pillars supported the pitched canopy of the porch, behind which the house had a multi-angled roof.

The garden was overgrown, although that didn't make it unattractive, there were flowering aloes and California poppies in among the invasive grasses, and in the middle of one section of the garden there was a flagpole bearing two flags, the stars and stripes and the flag of the Marine Corps. There was no sign of life from the house but were four cars parked in the driveway, including a white left hand drive 1950s English Morris Minor. I was surprised and impressed.

We went up to the front door, peered in through an adjacent window into what looked like a sort of waiting room. Around the side of the house there was an oil lamp and a set of artist's paint brushes resting on a low wall. We looked and we speculated, but there really wasn't much to see, and while we were doing this, I became aware that the next-door neighbour was sitting in his car in his driveway staring out at us, no doubt wondering what we were up to. He was a slight, middle-aged man wearing heavy sunglasses, which meant he had more anonymity than we did. I had no idea how long he'd been watching, nor whether he was on his way out or whether he'd just returned from an errand. Either way he'd decided to watch and wait, and keep an eye on us.

I don't think Anthony and I look very threatening, and if anybody had asked what we were up to we'd have said we were hardcore John Cage fans, which was true enough. The neighbour didn't get out of his car to approach us, but kept watching until we decided we'd seen enough or at least as much as we were likely to see. We decided to leave the house and walk around the rest of the neighborhood, which involved walking past the neighbour in his car. Seeing that we were leaving, he now got out of his vehicle, at which point we saw that he was wearing pyjamas under a bathrobe, and had carpet slippers on his feet. He wouldn't be doing much walking, and it was hard to believe he'd be performing errands. We nodded and smiled at him, and he smiled and nodded back, so we all went harmlessly on our way.

The houses in and around Moss Avenue tended to be long and low, with overhanging roofs, porches and gardens in the front, high fences protecting the gardens in the back. Some of the porches were completely open: people could see out, people could see in. Some of the gardens were simple but very well-tended, a few were fussy and overgrown, lots of potted plants, garden statues, whirligigs. One garden featured several stuffed toy monkeys tied to a tree.

Was there silence? No, of course not; there was the sound of kids playing unseen in backyards, one man was sawing the branches of a tree that overhung his front gate, there was the occasional passing car, the muted roar of the freeway, all elements that Cage might have employed in a composition. And at one moment, surprisingly, there was the sound of a piano coming from one of the houses. This was not Cagean, in fact the music sounded like Scott Joplin-style ragtime, being played perfectly well though without much verve. There was no way of seeing the player, and it could have been anyone of any age, but it was nice to imagine that this was the kind of thing the young John Cage might have played when he lived in Moss Avenue when he was learning the piano, and it was equally satisfying to imagine that this piano was being played by some young boy or girl who in the not too distant future would embrace experimentalism, and reinvent themselves.

42

It probably won't come as a great surprise if I tell you that Cage was a walker, and that he spent a lot of time walking in the woods, often collecting mushrooms. But it may surprise you – it did me – that he suffered from arthritis, which is a nightmare for walkers, as I've recently started to learn. Cage adopted a macrobiotic diet to help cure his condition, which probably worked as well as anything else ever does.

Discovering mushrooms while out walking is a great pleasure, and although the woods are no doubt the best place to find them, I also come across them in cities, growing in the grass verges in suburbs, in public parks. I have a few books that help to identify mushrooms and I used to carry one if I thought I was going to see mushrooms on my walks, but I stopped doing it. Although the books are perfectly good, and although I can usually identify the mushrooms with some degree of certainty, 'some degree' really isn't enough. It's the uncertainty that kills you.

I was once walking with my friend Hugh on Eltham Common, in South London. It was autumn and there were plenty of mushrooms around. By then I'd stopped even trying to identify them on my travels, but Hugh had an app on his phone, which claimed to do the job. The notion, which seemed quite novel at the time, now totally commonplace, was that you took a picture of the mushroom and zapped it through the app and an identification would come zapping back a few seconds later. Hugh took the picture and did as required. Nothing much happened. About forty minutes later, by which time we were a good long way from where we'd seen the mushrooms, the app returned an identification. No doubt the delay was caused by a weak phone system, but we speculated that that app connected with some poor lad in a dingy room somewhere who had a big encyclopedia of mushrooms to hand and that's how the identification was made. This didn't fill us with confidence.

No such doubts for John Cage, although he did once end up in hospital after mistaking hellebore for skunk cabbage on one of his foraging walks. And he did offer the observation that very few lion hunters are actually killed by lions, whereas a great many mushroom hunters are killed by mushrooms. I wonder how many walkers are killed by walking.

43

There's a section of Cage's text *Indeterminacy* (number 5) in which he talks about walking along and looking in the window of a stationery shop in which a mechanised pen was writing out the same penmanship exercises he'd learned as a child. But something had gone wrong with the mechanism, and although the pen continued to move, it now started tearing the paper to shreds and splattering ink everywhere.

This is the kind of thing walkers love, the kind of thing that makes a walk worthwhile, but the opening sentence of the piece really did surprise me. Cage writes, 'One evening I was walking along Hollywood Boulevard, nothing much to do.'

I can easily imagine Cage walking along Hollywood Boulevard. But I honestly can't imagine him walking there, or anywhere else, with 'nothing much to do'.

44

If you go on YouTube you can see John Cage performing 'Water Walk' a piece that involves him walking around a stage, performing various operations that make sound; with a bathtub full of water, ice cubes, a pressure cooker, a soda syphon and even a piano. It's part of an episode of the TV show 'I've Got a Secret' from 1960. The show's host is sceptical about the performance, but not downright hostile, and the audience finds it all hilarious.

Cage holds up very well, as you'd expect him to. When the host asks him to explain the title 'Water Walk', Cage says 'because it contains water and because I walk during the performance.' How can you not love this man?

45

I never went mushroom hunting with my dad, but we often went walking, and I do know that we once discussed mushrooms. I had discovered the fiction of H.G. Wells, an interest that's never quite gone away. He was one of the first 'grown up' writers I discovered more or less for myself, when I was about eleven years old. I read *The Invisible Man* and *The First Men in the Moon*, and I'd probably seen some version of these on TV or in the cinema, but the tipping point was that my dad had a copy of *The Time Machine* with a shiny silver cover and that was what really drew me. Yes, I judged a book by its cover.

My dad was in many ways an odd man. And one of his oddnesses was that he was absolutely sure that he knew things, even when it was quite clear, and it became increasingly clear, that he didn't. When he saw that I'd started reading Wells, he told me about *The History of Mr Polly*, which he said was a book about a man who grows poisonous mushrooms in his cellar and uses them to murder his wife. This sounds like a perfectly reasonable premise for a book, but it's not what happens in *The History of Mr Polly*, which I only read many, many years after my dad had talked about it, and it seems that he can't have read it at all.

It's possible that he meant a short story by Wells, titled 'The Purple Pileus', about a hapless, desperate and unhappily married shopkeeper named Coombes who walks away from his home and his job and goes into the pinewoods. There he finds what he thinks are poisonous mushrooms and he eats them in an attempt to kill himself, but they aren't poisonous in that sense, and he doesn't die. Instead, he's mystically transformed into a masterful and confident man, and his wife falls in love with him again. So, not at all as described by my dad, but you don't have to be much of a Freudian to wonder if this was what my dad really wanted, either to be dead or to be masterful, confident and adored by his wife.

46

You'll find Wells quoted (sometimes misquoted) in various places around the internet, both on straight-forward quotation websites, and also on those dubious 'advice to entry-level writers' sites, as having said or written, 'I write as I walk because I want to get some-where and I write as straight as I can, just as I walk as straight as I can, because that is the best way to get there.' It actually comes from *An Experiment in Autobiography*, and he says it in order to bad-mouth the prose style of Joseph Conrad, which he finds a bit fancy and over-literary.

The reasonable response to Wells's line is surely: well that all depends, doesn't it? Yes, a straight line is the shortest distance between two points, but if the two points are, say, either side of a river, it might be wise to walk along the riverbank to a bridge rather than just striding straight through the water. There's also the matter that you don't need to be some fancy pants flâneur to believe that walking isn't always about getting somewhere quickly and efficiently. Even mere mortals recognise that a slow meandering walk without an obvious goal is sometimes much more enjoyable than going in a straight line from one place to another.

I'm not even all that persuaded by 'straightness' as a virtue in writing either, but I think Wells had a point, given the kind of books he wrote. If you're going to write fanciful stuff, 'scientific romance' about time travel, invisibility, dubious experiments in vivisection and a war of the worlds, then a good plain prose style helps a lot with establishing credibility and suspension of disbelief.

47

In fact, there's some evidence that Wells didn't always walk the walk quite as purposefully as he claimed.

In Jerome K. Jerome's *My Life and Times*, he describes a trip he made to see Wells who was living in Folkestone at the time. Jerome had been under the weather and Wells invited him down to the coast for some sea air and a rest. It was not restful.

Jerome writes, 'To "rest" in the neighbourhood of Wells is like curling yourself up and trying to go to sleep in the centre of a cyclone.' Wells took him walking at speed up the hills of the South Downs, talking manically all the time. Then on the Sunday evening there was a hurricane with driving sleet, but Wells was sure a walk would do the pair of them good.

'We'll all have a blow,' said Wells, as they set off.

48

Life being as it is, I immediately came across an anecdote told by architect Frank Lloyd Wright, which suggests he took a different view about walking from that espoused by Wells.

Wright was nine years old, there was snow on the ground and he went walking with a no-nonsense uncle. After they'd crossed a snow-covered field the uncle stopped and looked back at their footsteps, observing young Frank's tracks wandered aimlessly from the fence to the cattle to the woods and back again, whereas the uncle's tracks were dead straight. The uncle thought there was an important lesson here, but Wright learned quite a different lesson from the one his uncle had in mind, one that changed his outlook on life. 'I determined right then, not to miss most things in life, as my uncle had.' Wright became a meanderer.

I've walked around, in one sense or another, quite a few Frank Lloyd Wright buildings. The Hollyhock House and the Ennis House were both close to where I lived in Los Angeles. The Hollyhock house was in the middle of a public space, Barnsdall Park, conceived by Aline Barnsdall to be an artists' colony on Hollywood Boulevard. Well, you can imagine how that turned out. When I knew it, it was rarely open to the public, largely because lumps were often falling off it, caused by earth tremors, but you could always walk around the perimeter and admire the building – variously described as Mayan or Egyptian, or, by Wright himself as 'California Romanza', which in this case means great slabby concrete walls, terraces, stylised mouldings that resemble hollyhocks somewhat, but not very much.

I think Wright never walked around the completed Ennis House, about a mile and a half due north of the Hollyhock. He fell out with his client and his son took over. It appears in *House on Haunted Hill* and in *Bladerunner*. It's not especially scary or futuristic, but rather huge, solid, forbidding, and in the real world on a perfectly ordinary suburban street. I did walk around it on one of their open days when I went for a tour. I parked my car in the wrong place, and got told off. I should have gone on foot: it was walking distance away from where I lived.

49

There's a joke, a one-liner from the deadpan comedian Stephen Wright, who specialises in one-liners. He says, 'Everywhere's walking distance if you have enough time.'

But I don't think this is actually true. Regardless of how much time you've got, New York isn't walkable from London, any more than it's drivable.

Here's another one. This is from Billy Connolly, 'Before you judge a man, walk a mile in his shoes. After that who cares? You're a mile away and you've got his shoes.'

Of course, depending on the size and type of shoe, you might find it very difficult indeed to walk even a couple of hundred yards. Or you might find it OK to walk a mile in them, but a mile really isn't very far, and after two miles you might be crippled.

50

At this point in literary history a lot of people know the story of Samuel Beckett's shoes.

Georges Pelorson, who was a friend of Samuel Beckett's, recalled that they walked together in Phoenix Park, Dublin in 1929 or 1930, when Beckett was twenty-three or twenty-four. After they'd gone a few hundred yards, Pelerson noticed that Beckett was walking like a duck, and asked if his feet were hurting, and Beckett said yes, his shoes were too tight. Pelorson asked why he didn't change the shoes, but it was a few years before he got an answer.

Pelorson met Beckett in Paris with James Joyce, and both Beckett and Joyce were wearing identical bright yellow shoes. Not only was Beckett wearing shoes of the same style as Joyce, he was wearing shoes of the same size, even though his feet were bigger.

I find this pretty odd. Beckett was a young man in the early 1930s, but not *that* young. And although I understand some forms of hero worship, I'm not sure that wearing shoes which happen to be the same size as one's hero, is really very worshipful.

Joyce did however write in *Ulysses* what I think is one of the truly great statements about walking: 'We walk through ourselves, meeting robbers, ghosts, giants, old men, young men, wives, widows, brothers-in-law. But always meeting ourselves.'

51

One more joke: it's about moon walking. There's a story that when the crew of Apollo 11 were discussing what the first words of a man on the moon should be, Michael Collins, the pilot of the command module, said to Neil Armstrong, 'If you had any balls, you'd say "Oh my, God, what is that thing?" then scream and cut your mic.'

It's a good line, and of course Collins was the poor sod who knew he wasn't going to get to walk on the moon, so his humour may have been that much edgier. And I assume Armstrong was the kind of man who could take a joke. If you told Buzz Aldrin that he didn't have the balls, you'd end up with a face full of knuckles.

52

I like rocks. I know very little about geology, but if I'm out walking and I see a rock at my feet and I like the look of it, then I pick it up and take it away with me.

Of course the question of what it means to 'like the look' of a rock is a tricky one, and I've thought about why one rock appeals more than another. It's obviously got something to do with general aesthetics but it's also about personal taste (I'm especially fond of flint and obsidian) and maybe it's also to do with pareidolia – things that look like other things. Everybody likes a rock that looks like an animal or a face, or at least not wholly like a rock.

However, if you're on a long walk and you pick up every rock you like the look of, you'll end up carrying half a ton of geological samples in your pockets and rucksack. So my technique (call it that) is to pick up the first rock I like and carry it with me until I see another rock that l like better, then I pick that one up and drop the first.

It's not a very sophisticated process, I never made any great claims for the originality of this practice, but I'd also never met anybody else who did it until I was in Quartzsite, Arizona, one hell of a town, a desert outpost, a centre for rock and fossil hunters, and depending on the day and time of year, you can find any number of dealers there selling rocks, most of which I think they've picked up while walking in the desert. I understand this is perfectly legal in those parts, though it's definitely not in some other parts of the United States.

Buying rocks from a dealer has always seemed a bit of a cheat to me, but of course if the dealer is a local, and a hands-on kind of a guy, he has all the time in the world to go hunting for rocks in the desert, finding really good stuff, whereas I've only ever been a tourist passing through those parts. So the dealer has much 'better' rocks.

I got talking to one of these dealers and, without any prompting from me, he said that sometimes when he was walking in the desert, for pleasure rather than business, his method was just the same as mine – go out there, pick up a rock, keep it until you find a better one, then swap it. I can't say I felt like I'd found a kindred soul, but it was somehow very cheering.

53

I found a theoretical fellow traveller in Richard Long, specifically a text piece titled 'Walking Stones'. It states, in bold capitals, that he walked across England from the Atlantic Coast to North Sea Coast, picking up a stone every day and carrying it with him till the next day when he put it down and picked up another, 'and so on from day to day from stone to stone.'

The walks covered 382 miles in eleven days, 'FROM A FIRST PEBBLE ON WELCOMBE MOUTH BEACH TO THE LAST STONE THROWN INTO THE SEA AT LOWESTOFT.'

The artwork is the panel of text on the wall, though obviously the text wouldn't exist if it weren't for the walk. Incidentally Google maps clocks this walk at 329 miles, but why quibble? Walking this kind of distance in eleven days strikes me as very impressive — about thirty miles a day – but I do wonder how he selected the stones he picked up. Was it based on aesthetic choice or random selection or something else? You might also wonder at what point does a stone become a pebble, or indeed a rock.

In the end, Long ended up with no rocks at all in his pockets or rucksack because he threw the last one into the sea. I, on the other hand, often end up taking at least one home with me. In the end of course, I often get rid of these too. Over the years I must have dispersed hundreds of rocks, some of them a very long way from where they started. I know there was a rock with a fossil in it that I found while walking in Morocco which ended up on a beach where I was walking in Suffolk. This wasn't exactly a work of art, but I probably wouldn't have done it if it hadn't been for Richard Long.

54

In Chichibu, in Japan, there is, or anyway used to be, a museum named Chinsekikan, literally 'hall of curious rocks', although all the rocks here have a specific curiosity. They resemble human faces, and all are naturally occurring, they haven't been altered or turned into art. They were the collection of the late Shozo Hayama who spent fifty years walking around picking up facially anthropomorphic rocks. At first, he picked them up to sell on to rock dealers, but then he decided to keep them for himself.

There are at least 1700 specimens in the collection. I like this idea very much, but sometimes I don't trust the human capacity to find things that resemble other things – the pareidolia I mentioned. One of my minor curatorial fantasies is to set up a small museum of rocks that look exactly and only like rocks.

55

I'm well aware of the eco tourist mantra, 'Leave only footprints, take only photographs', which gets attributed to Chief Seattle of the Suquamish tribe. If that's accurate – and I don't think it is given that the Chief's dates were 1786–1866 – he was way ahead of the game.

I have no real argument with the chief, or anyone else, about this. Obviously I'm not in favour of driving a truck into the desert and loading it up with tons of rock specimens, and hauling them away, but if you're walking in some scrubby bit of territory, outside any kind of designated park or preserve, and you find a horse bone or a lump of quartz lying in your path, well I don't think it's the crime of the century to pick it up and take it home with you.

Out in the wild or on a beach, it's a thing that many people do, but I also tend to be a bit of a scavenger when I walk in cities. No guilt here. I think it's perfectly okay to pick up just about any old thing that's lying around in the street. I've picked up toys, a loudspeaker, hubcaps, a knife that looked like a murder weapon, on one occasion a couple of volumes of an encyclopedia. I could claim I was picking up litter, beautifying the environment, though it was never really that.

The question then arises of what you actually do with all these disjecta when you get them home. For years I've been accumulating stuff and putting it in various spare rooms and sheds, and my garage. And I suppose there was always some idea in the back of my mind that I might become an outsider artist, a junk sculptor like Noah Purifoy, or one of those curator-artists like Mark Dion, both of whom I admire greatly. If all those items I'd collected had been put in a display case or a vitrine, they'd certainly have gained in status, might have become a major art installation.

But the years go by and the sculpture doesn't get made, and yes I suppose any accumulation involves a kind of curating, but I don't see the good folks from the Pitt Rivers museum knocking at my door, asking me to install a display of the Nicholson Scavenger Collection, and so once in a while I thin and distill the archive, which is perhaps better described as throwing away the junk I've picked, which is, in general, a remarkably pleasurable experience.

56

My pal and walking companion Anthony Miller performs a specialised kind of scavenging. He's a bookish man and he says he's only interested in scavenging things written or printed on paper. If he sees a flyer or a postcard or a shopping list lying on the pavement or in the gutter, he knows he's in business. He swoops. His dream of course is to find a discarded notebook that contains some perfect and previously unknown Dadaist poetry. It's an unrealistic dream if you ask me, but a noble one.

Anthony now has a wife and a three-year-old daughter, and his scavenging has been much curtailed, at least when he's out with the family. Comments from his wife such as, 'Don't pick that up, that's what hobos do,' 'Put it down, you don't know where it's been,' 'Why would you bring that into the house?' have deterred him considerably.

When he's walking along with his daughter, she's intensely attracted to anything shiny, but he remains a purist. He still only goes for paper.

57

I accept that for some people walking is an abstract, immaterial activity without any end product. You go out, you come back, and although you may be changed or uplifted or enlightened, you haven't made or acquired anything. Unless, of course, your walk involves scavenging or shopping, or if you're an assemblage artist or a surrealist.

In the 1960s, '70s and early '80s Harry Smith, best known to me as an avant-garde filmmaker, walked the streets of Manhattan picking up discarded paper planes. He annotated them with the time and place they were found and formed a considerable collection that made it into the Smithsonian Institution.

Well before that, in the 1920s, just about the time Smith was born, Joseph Cornell also walked the streets of New York 'combing through jumbles of objects' as his biographer Deborah Solomon puts it. At the same time, she says, André Breton was acquiring surrealist objects from Paris flea markets. In *L'Amour fou* (1936), Breton described his practice as 'wandering in search of everything.' I suppose the great thing about searching for everything is that wherever you go, you find what you're looking for.

In 1942, Breton and a few other surrealists were in New York and were not much impressed by the city. They went to galleries and movies and walked down Third Avenue with Breton pointing out 'surreal' objects in the shop windows.

Cornell and Breton did meet – Cornell organised a showing of some 'nickelodeon classics'. And, according to Solomon, the surrealists regarded Cornell himself as a kind of surrealist object, 'a passive autodidact who wandered the city with a brown shopping bag full of trouvailles.'

Breton's collecting was intense and various, though much of it ethnological: Katchina dolls, African fetish items, materials from the Pacific Northwest, folk art, but also found objects, coins and of course surrealist artworks. A wall of his apartment and its collection has been preserved in the Centre Pompidou. Of course, these things were not found on the streets, but a good amount of wandering and looking and searching was no doubt involved in their acquisition. Most sources say the collection contained 5,300 items, others have it higher.

Certainly the auction catalogue produced when the bulk of the collection was sold off in 2003 runs to eight fat volumes. I know this because I laid hands on a set when I happened to be staying in the *Daily Telegraph* flat in Paris. Did you know the *Daily Telegraph* had a flat in Paris? I didn't. And there on a bookshelf was the eight-volume set.

I thought very seriously about stealing them, but I didn't a) because of my own moral compass, though that was probably the least of the reasons, b) because I thought somebody might notice it had gone, and I didn't want to be pursued by the *Daily Telegraph* and/ or the French police, and perhaps most important of all, c) because the volumes were immensely heavy and I would have had to carry them on my long walk to the station to get a train back to England.

I see that catalogue currently sells for a few hundred pounds and I don't know if that makes me feel better or worse.

58

The kind of walking and scavenging that Anthony and I do, the kind that rock hunters do, the kind that Cornell and Breton did, always involves a process of selection. You choose one thing and reject another. In the art world this might be known as 'curation'. But what happens if you decide not to select, but to allow your scavenging to be essentially random?

And so we come to Francis Alÿs, the Belgian artist, who has created quite a few great pieces of walking art. The first one I ever became aware of was titled 'The Collector' from 1990. Alÿs made a crude toy dog, on wheels, no more that a foot long. The McGuffin was that the body was magnetised, so that as Alÿs pulled it through the streets of Mexico City, where he lived at the time, it picked up, attracted, retained little bits of scrap metal that were lying on the ground, with no act of selection on his part.

He said in a 2011 interview: 'After three days people started talking about the crazy gringo walking around with his magnetised dog, but after seven days, the story, the anecdote, had remained even though the characters were gone.'

Personally, I'd be very embarrassed and self-conscious if I was pulling a magnetic toy dog through the streets. I would have been much more at ease with a 1994 work Alÿs did titled 'Magnetic Shoes'. For this he ditched the dog and magnetised his own footwear. This time the city was Havana and the piece was created, performed, for a Havana Biennial. A video shows Alÿs walking the streets, determinedly though casually, until he finally gets back to his hotel, his shoes caked in detritus.

In a different interview, this one with Russell Ferguson, Alÿs says, 'Walking, in particular drifting, or strolling, is already – within the speed culture of our time – a kind of resistance. Paradoxically it's also the last private space, safe from the phone or e-mail … It's a state where you can be both alert to all that happens in your peripheral vision and hearing, and yet totally lost in your thought process.'

I have no argument with that beyond the obvious fact that as I walk the streets these days, I see a great many people who are very much not safe from their phone or email.

59

Alÿs is one of a whole slew of people who make art out of walking, and in some cases call themselves walking artists. Inevitably I find some much more interesting than others. Richard Long (of course, op. cit.), Hamish Fulton, Sophie Calle, are among my favourites.

Richard Long is sometimes considered a 'land artist' whose works may involve simply stamping out a pattern on the ground or rearranging elements in a landscape, but these works are often made as the result of epic walks, in distant and inhospitable parts of the world.

Long's pupil and fellow traveller Hamish Fulton insists he's a walking artist, not a land artist, though the landscape is always involved. In 1973, he had an epiphany while walking 1,022 miles in forty-seven days from Duncansby Head in Scotland (near John O'Groats) to Lands End in the far southwest of England, and decided thereafter to 'only make art resulting from the experience of individual walks'. His motto: 'No walk no art.'

Sophie Calle followed, or stalked, a strange (or at least unknown) man from Paris to Venice, and documented the process with photographs, maps and texts, in the 'Venetian Suite'. For months she'd followed strangers in the street, photographing them without their knowledge, or indeed consent, until she lost sight of them as they disappeared into the crowd.

Then, in January 1980, in Paris, she briefly followed a man, who as usual went out of sight, but that very evening she was introduced to him at an art opening. During their conversation, he told her he was about to visit Venice, so she decided to follow him. This went on for thirteen days, and at one point the man, known as Henri B., spotted her and they went for a walk together. In the end, she followed him all the way back to Paris.

60

Once when I was in New York I met a couple, an American woman and an English man, and I asked them how they'd met. The story was that he'd been following her as she walked through the streets of Manhattan, and when she realised, she turned, confronted him and demanded, 'Are you following me?'

And he replied in his cut glass (and to my ears slightly affected, phony-sounding) English accent, 'I'd like to deny it, but I can't. You're too beautiful, too perfect and I could never lie to you.'

She fell for it. It was the start of a beautiful, or at least functioning, relationship. I suspect it wouldn't have worked with every English accent. I'm not sure it would work with any English accent today, but I could be wrong.

I think I can safely say I have never followed anybody through the streets.

61

There's an art piece by Marina Abramovic, from 1988, titled 'The Lovers: The Great Wall Walk'. Abramovic and her then boyfriend Ulay decided to mark the end of their relationship with an art performance (the way you do), setting off from the two ends of the Great Wall of China, and walking for ninety days until they met up in Shaanxi province. There they were to have one final embrace and go their separate ways forever. Better than doing it by text message, no doubt.

Now, I am not a walking artist or a performance artist, but I do know a little about break ups, and I think that if I'd been Ulay I wouldn't have played along with this. Or rather I think I might have *pretended* to play along, but then stayed right where I was – Ulay was actually at the western end of the Wall on the edge of the Gobi Desert, a pleasant enough spot I imagine – and

I'd have hung around there until La Abramovic arrived, perhaps 180 days later. I might have said, 'Hey kid, you're the art superstar who uses endurance as an essential part of her artistic praxis!'

But Ulay did play along, at least at the time. I understand there have been recent meetings, and Ulay has sued Abramovic for non-payment of proceeds from their earlier joint works of art.

62

There's a short film by Charlotte Prodger (who won the 2018 Turner Prize), titled *LHB*, from 2017, which begins with footage of the Torness nuclear power station in Scotland while a voice over by Prodger discusses her 'obsession' with the Pacific Crest Trail (PCT), a serious and popular hiking trail that runs over two and a half thousand miles between the Canadian and Mexican borders. The film continues with readings from the blogs of two hikers on the PCT, who are, we're told, both queer women. Then the voiceover discusses the editing principles involved in gay pornography, and then there's footage of Prodger taking a piss or two while out hiking.

Interviewed about the film, Prodger said, 'I walk a lot. You've got to piss. I piss outside a lot. I like it … I always like thinking about my body in relationship to landscape in that way. I had been filming it for a while. Me and Cassie [her girlfriend] would be walking together and I'd say, "I'm going for a piss," and then I'd say, "Oh can you film it?"'

This found its way into *Private Eye*'s 'Pseud's Corner', which struck me as just a little unfair. We all need to pee while out walking, and it's much easier in the countryside than in the town. As Jeff Goldblum's character Michael says in *The Big Chill*, 'That's the great thing about the outdoors; it's one giant toilet.'

63

I'm well aware that there's a terrible biological, and practical, unfairness in the comparative anatomy of male and female urinary arrangements. It's so easy for a man to go behind a tree, do his business and move on, but women have to do far more negotiating, undressing, squatting, wiping and dressing again.

I once appeared on a radio show for the BBC, *Ramblings* with Clare Balding, the well-known horse-woman, broadcaster, journalist, memoirist and all-round national treasure. We walked in coastal Suffolk. It took a good many hours for us to discuss, among other things, walking, landscape and the many different words we have for different kinds of walking. All this was effort-lessly guided, directed and recorded by the producer Lucy Lunt. It was a good walk, a long one. It made for a long day, and we were outdoors all of the time.

At one point I did have to make my mannish excuses and go behind a convenient tree to relieve myself. And eventually Clare Balding had to go too. Being a national treasure, she was reluctant just to let rip in the open air – you can imagine what the papers would have made of it if somebody had spotted her.

As it happened, we'd got to Dunwich by then and were close to a pub, so the producer and I suggested that if Clare went in there they'd surely be happy to let her use their facilities even if she didn't buy a drink. She thought about it and calculated that if she did go in, she'd have to explain what she was doing, why she was there, who she was with and so on. She'd have to have a chat, maybe sign an autograph, perhaps pose for pictures, generally be a celebrity. It all seemed far too much trouble. She went behind a bush instead.

She did not say, 'Oh can you film it?', but then I never expected her to.

64

The great artist John Baldessari died in 2020, which seemed a great shame, even though he was 88. I didn't know him, but I knew people who did. He was not, in the usual sense, a 'walking artist'. He's generally considered to be a 'conceptual artist' with all the contradictions that involves, but walking sometimes featured in his works, as in 'Walking Forward-Running Past', 1971.

It's a thirteen-minute video, its images deliberately crude, some stills, some moving, showing Baldessari both walking and running. The New York Met says, 'By creating a video with still images, Baldessari urges viewers to question notions of sequence and cinematic time, and how we depict the past, present, and future.' Well, yes, isn't that what we all question as we walk?

Another Baldessari piece is 'A Movie: Directional Piece Where People Are Walking', 1972–1973. In fact, it's not a movie but a set of twenty-two black and white still photographs of people walking, with circles of acrylic paint over their faces.

And there's also 'Walking the Plank', 1988, again acrylic on black and white photographs, but just two this time, each show a man and a plank, on one the man's kneeling, on the other he's walking, or at least standing up, though in fact he looks as though he's about to fall off, which I suppose is what walking the plank always involves. Again, the faces, or heads, are concealed behind bright circles of paint.

Baldessari once complained that he'd be forever known as 'the guy who puts dots over people's faces,' but there are worse things to be known as.

65

I'm not trying to assert any great kinship with John Baldessari, but we did have one thing in common: we both taught at CalArts (California Institute of the Arts), in Valencia, an hour or so up the road from LA, though we taught there at very different times and with very different results. He was there, 1970 to 1986; I was there about thirty years after he left. He was well loved; I was not.

One of Baldessari's artistic, educational strategies involved having a student throw a dart into a map of Los Angeles, and then the class would all go there and spend the day, taking pictures and shooting film and video. That sounds like a process that involves some walking, but I assume they didn't walk all the way to the place where the dart pierced the map, but rather they drove, then did their walking around when they got there. I have also read that Baldessari described this strategy as 'fucking about'.

I think my time at Cal Arts would have been much more enjoyable if I'd done more fucking about. As it was, I took things rather too seriously. I was teaching creative writing in the Faculty of Critical Studies. Oh god, I know. I did try to incorporate some walking into my pedagogic method, without much success. I sometimes walked around the small campus with one or two of the students to whom I was supposedly offering pastoral support, and that was just fine. And I did once think about offering to teach a course at the college to be titled 'Psychogeographies: The Poetry and Politics of Walking and Writing', but in the end it seemed it'd be like hard and thankless work.

Mostly, while teaching, I felt I was involved in some terrible Ponzi scheme, teaching creative writing to people who, with few exceptions, were never going to be professional or even very competent writers. For the good ones, their best chance of making a living would be to get a job in a college teaching creative writing to people who, with few exceptions, were never going to be professional or even very competent writers. And so on.

Given the way things are these days in American colleges, with students regarding themselves as clients, customers and consumers, determined to get their money's worth, I think a teacher who did too much, possibly any 'fucking about' would very quickly get fired. I'm sure it was best just to walk away, as I did.

66

I believe the greatest exit line ever delivered by a walker
was 'I'm just going outside and may be some time' said
by Captain Lawrence Oates, part of the British Terra
Nova expedition that went to the South Pole, but arrived
only after Amundsen. In fact, there's some doubt about
whether Oates actually said those words, but when in
doubt, print the legend.

After their 'failure' they then faced an 895-mile
trek back to base. The team was not in good shape and
Oates, who was suffering from frostbite and gangrenous
feet, suggested that they put him in a sleeping bag and
leave him out in the snow. They refused to do that, but
early the next morning, 16 March 1912, Oates delivered
his famous words and went out into the blizzard. They
didn't stop him.

Another member of the crew was Edward Wilson,

who was an alumnus of my old college, Gonville and Caius, Cambridge. There was a print of him in the college library and when I first saw it his name was completely unfamiliar to me. I now know that he was a naturalist, that he studied medicine, became a doctor, suffered from tuberculosis, but nevertheless felt fit enough to sign up for the Antarctic expedition.

Apsley Cherry-Garrard, who was part of the support team for the expedition, and later author of *The Worst Journey in the World* about the expedition, said that Wilson was not a particularly strong man, that he was slim and lightly built, with just a 36-inch chest, but a great walker.

Cherry-Garrard writes that he was an ideal example of his contention, 'that it is not strength of body but rather strength of will which carries a man farthest.' I don't doubt that this is true of many of the world's great walkers.

67

Long before I taught at Cal Arts, I was, very briefly, a teacher of drama at a college of further education in Weybridge, Surrey. I'd done no teacher training, and I found the job very hard indeed. On Thursday nights, after a long day, I went to the pub where a few of the other teachers, perhaps they called themselves lecturers, gathered and complained about how terrible it was to be a teacher, in an attempt to reassure me.

I only ever stayed for a couple of drinks because I lived miles away, all the way across London, and I had to take a couple of trains to get home. One night as I was walking soberly along the cinder path between the college and the railway station, a path that nobody else was using at that moment, I looked up and saw a long, bright, whitish thing moving slowly in the sky above the trees. It didn't look like a plane or a helicopter or weather balloon: if anything, it looked like a glowing airborne submarine.

It was undoubtedly an unidentified flying object in the sense that it was an object, it was flying, and I definitely couldn't identify it. It was a strange and unsettling sight but it wasn't at all scary or threatening. It was just a thing that happened to be there. I walked along looking up at it and after a short while it wasn't there anymore, and I continued on my way to the station.

It wasn't a dramatic or life-changing experience, and it certainly didn't change my beliefs or ideas about aliens, because I really didn't have any, but obviously the event has stayed with me precisely because it remains unexplained. It's probably the oddest experience I've ever had while walking, and in some ways one of the most reassuring. The aliens in the craft, if there were aliens in the craft, were not the killer extraterrestrials of legend. They were happy enough to let a man walk along a cinder path to the railway station.

It was the kind of experience that might almost make a man happy to be a teacher.

68

One of the walking anecdotes I tell rather too often is of walking with my father when I was a boy, and we came to a wood and a sign saying 'Private. No Trespassing'. My dad was the kind of man who assumed that signs and warnings applied to everybody but him, and so we walked on, ignoring the sign, and were eventually confronted by the landowner on horseback, who wasn't happy to see us there and said this was his garden and how would we feel if he came and rode his horse in our garden?

We lived in a council house in Sheffield at the time, so the prospect would have been quite surreal, but frankly I'd have liked to see it. I didn't say that. I didn't say anything. And like all the best confrontations this one petered out without any great conflict. We walked back. He rode on.

Years afterwards I found something oddly similar in a short story by PG Wodehouse, who I believe was an enthusiastic walker. The story is 'The Autograph Hunters', and describes one Mr Watson, walking through the wood that's part of his property, and finding a boy trespassing there. 'He was not a man who was fond of boys even in their proper place, and the sight of one in the middle of his wood, prancing lightly about among the nesting pheasants, stirred his never too placid mind to its depths'.

Of course, this was a boy on his own, which is quite a different matter from a boy with his father. Good Yorkshireman and Yorkshire boy that we were, I think it's safe to say that my dad and I were not 'prancing lightly about among the nesting pheasants.' At the time I wouldn't even have known what a pheasant looked like.

69

Also in Wodehouse I found a wonderful description of walking in art galleries, from 'The Rummy Affair of Old Biffy', written in 1924, though it seems like it could have been written this morning. The narrator is Bertie Wooster:

> Well, you know, I have never been much of a lad for exhibitions … The citizenry in the mass always rather puts me off, and after I have been shuffling along with the multitude for a quarter of an hour or so I feel as if I were walking on hot bricks.

I spend a fair amount of time in galleries and museums, and of course visiting them usually involves walking, but the walking that I and everybody else does in museums and galleries has nothing much to do with the way we walk in 'real life'.

This form of art or culture walking is ponderous, thoughtful, heavy, a way of showing that you're a serious person and taking the art seriously. And, of course, it's not real walking, you walk for a bit then you stand for a bit, you take a step back to get a broader view, then take a couple of steps forward to peer at the wall texts, then walk on. You shuffle from one exhibit to the next, then you walk into the next room in the gallery, and so on, feeling relief when you get to the end and can have a sit down in the café. Unlike Wooster, I can do an hour rather than fifteen minutes, but I believe that an hour of walking round an art gallery is probably, in terms of weariness and aching feet, the equivalent of a three-hour walk in the street.

70

Walking around art in the great outdoors, say at the Yorkshire Sculpture Park or Storm King Art Centre in upstate New York – both of which claim to cover 500 acres – makes for a less footsore experience it seems to me. It's not as easy as going for a walk in the countryside, but it's easier than slogging round a gallery.

Both Yorkshire Sculpture Park and Storm King feature, or at least have featured, work by Andy Goldsworthy, not a walking artist per se though a man whose work must involve him in a fair bit of walking as he tramps through various landscapes creating 'environmental' art, sometimes using leaves or twigs, wool or bracken, though at other times using stones and rocks to create more solid and permanent structures such as cairns and faux sheepfolds. Sometimes he even employs professional dry stone wallers.

At a rather grim, and let's say transitional, point in my life I found myself unemployed and with no hope of making a living as a writer, and living back in Sheffield, having been away for well over a decade. I walked down to the job centre, to save bus fare, and they offered me two options: to be a casual sprout picker in Lincolnshire or an apprentice dry stone waller.

I've often thought how different, and possibly better, my life would have been if I'd done the apprenticeship (the sprout picking was obviously a non-starter). I'd have liked working outdoors, and would obviously have liked the walking, and maybe Andy Goldsworthy would have spotted my talent and signed me up. I'm sure dry stone walling must play havoc with the joints, the hands, the knees, the back, giving you arthritis at the very least. The English environment is not always welcoming, and it may not just be a matter of the weather.

71

If you're a writer who walks, people will from time to time ask you, sometimes even pay you, to write about walking, whether in the form of a book review, a listicle, or in the case below a preface. I was asked out of the blue to write an introductory essay for Torbjørn Ekelund's *In Praise of Paths*. I said yes without much hesitation and was happy to find it's a really good book.

One interesting side effect caused by that title and the use of the word 'path' was that for a while as I wandered through the world, I constantly asked myself, 'Is this really a path I'm walking on?' Sometimes the answer was an unequivocal yes, and on some occasions, I was walking on a special *kind* of path: a footpath, a garden path, a tow path, a bridle path.

But at other times the question got more complicated. I asked myself, was I perhaps walking on a trail or a track, along a lane or a pedestrian way or a desire line, a ginnel, a snicket, a twitten. I found myself wondering whether these were types of paths, or whether they were physically and philosophically something quite different, perhaps not paths at all.

Well, I didn't come to any hard and fast answers to these questions, and fortunately, Torbjørn Ekelund didn't either, but perhaps my occasional puzzlement was an indication that a path is not such a simple thing as it first appears, or as many would suppose, which is to say that a path is rarely 'just' a path. Yes, it may be a means of getting from A to B (or Z), but it can very often be metaphorical or allegorical as well. Ekelund points out that if you Google the word 'path' you'll 'have to scroll through countless religious or spiritual references, pages about yoga, meditation, mindfulness, everything other than a physical path.'

Ekelund's range of reference went outside the usual suspects. I was introduced to a lot of unfamiliar, generally Scandinavian, figures, such as Bjørn Amsrud, the first person to walk the length of Norway, the philosopher Arne Næss who regularly hiked to his mountaintop cabin, but always went by a different route. I was especially fascinated by Joshua French, a Norwegian mercenary jailed in the Democratic Republic of Congo, who spent every day of his incarceration walking back and forth along a corridor that was only fifty feet long.

There are two pieces of Ekelund wisdom that have lived with me. First, that 'The history of the path is the history of us,' and secondly, 'The path is order in chaos.' Words to live by, and words by which to lose and find yourself.

72

I don't know Simon Armitage and he doesn't know me, but I owe him a favour. He was in the bookshop at the Yorkshire Sculpture Park, saw my book *The Lost Art of Walking* on sale there, bought it, and presumably liked it because when he was curating some events at the Off the Shelf festival in Sheffield, I was invited to conduct a walk, which I duly did. We have still never met, although he's gone on to considerably greater things, including becoming Poet Laureate. In turn I was asked to review his book *Walking Home: A Poet's Journey* for the *San Francisco Chronicle*.

The book describes a walk along the Pennine Way, the rugged 256-mile trail that runs along the spine of England. This is by no means untrodden territory, but Armitage has a special connection. He grew up in the village of Marsden in West Yorkshire, toward the southern end of the trail, a suitable first stop for walkers doing the route south to north, and he remembers as a boy seeing mud-splattered hikers emerging from the hills after completing a single day's trek. Some of them gave up at this point, but Armitage is made of sterner stuff, and as he walks the route the 'wrong', or at least less usual, way, from north to south, he is literally and metaphorically walking home.

To make life more complicated for himself, and more interesting for the reader, he gives a poetry reading at the end of each day's walk, in a pub or school or village hall or anywhere else that will have him, passing the hat round at the end of his performance and also relying on the kindness of strangers to give him a bed for the night. 'So, it's basically 256 miles of begging,' he writes.

There are also accounts of his poetry readings, the good gigs as well as the bad, and inevitably the latter are much more fun to read about; though in general he finds audiences who are remarkably (and perhaps surprisingly) receptive and generous. There's a flashback to a supremely uncomfortable and hilarious gig he once did in a city-centre art gallery when a man in a doughnut costume appeared in the street and leaned against the glass front wall of the gallery. As the house manager of the event tried to move the doughnut man along, he protested, 'Doughnuts can like poetry.' Oh, but can they like walking?

73

I wish somebody had asked me to review Lauren
Elkin's *Flâneuse: Women Walk the City in Paris, New
York, Tokyo, Venice and London*, but nobody did, and it
eventually became obvious that I wasn't going to be
sent a freebie despite my appearance in the bibliog-
raphy. So I went out and bought a copy, which I was
happy to do.

I wanted the book to be good – I like walking, I like
women, I like women who walk, and I want women to
be able to walk wherever they choose without being
abused or threatened. Hell, some of my best friends are
flâneuses.

There's no denying there's a terrible unfairness
about the difficulties and dangers that women face
while walking. True, even the bravest man occasionally
finds himself in a place he'd rather not be, encountering

people he'd rather not meet, but however bad it may be for men, it's likely to be worse for women.

That doesn't, of course, mean there are no women walkers, as Elkin proves in her book: Virginia Woolf, Martha Gellhorn, Deborah Levy, Jean Rhys, Germaine Krull, are among those celebrated.

I very much liked Elkin's description of living in Tokyo, where she didn't have the very best time. 'What bothered me most was the certainty I felt that there was a great city out there full of places I wanted to discover, but I didn't know where to look for them. I didn't know what there was out there. I didn't know where to go, where to walk.'

Well, this is a feeling many of us have had, often in places much less unfamiliar than Tokyo, but my own limited experience of walking in Tokyo suggests that it's impossible to walk a hundred yards there without encountering some intriguing wonder, whether you're looking for it or not. Of course, you don't see everything, and of course you miss things, but wherever you are there's always something amazing and inscrutable.

74

I assume Lauren Elkin had a map, but perhaps she needed a better one than she had. However, I don't think anybody has ever had a map anywhere near as good as the one described by Beryl Markham in *West with the Night*, 1942, a book about her travels in what was then British East Africa, now Kenya. She writes, 'A map says to you ... "I am the earth in the palm of your hand. Without me, you are alone and lost."'

Well, you can certainly be alone and lost without a map, but in Tokyo you can be very alone and lost even with one. When I was there, I always carried a map with me, but I never felt as though I had the earth in the palm of my hand; mostly I felt as though I was carrying a rather useless piece of paper. Sometimes, inevitably, I was also consulting a rather useless graphic on a cell phone screen. True, given the dense population of Tokyo, I was rarely alone, but a lot of the time I was lost. It was some consolation that I frequently saw locals on the street, also staring at maps, and looking just as lost and confused as I was.

One of the many things I hadn't expected in Tokyo were the free maps that seemed to be given away everywhere, and I picked them up whenever I could. I still have the majority of them in my 'archive'.

Most of the maps I picked up, of course, were just tourist maps whose main reason for existing wasn't to help travelers go wherever they pleased, but to direct them to some very specific places, i.e. the businesses that had paid to have advertisements on the back of these maps. This was a plain enough illustration that maps are always in somebody's interest, and that these interests may not necessarily be the same as yours, though of course if you're looking for a nearby sushi restaurant then these interests may coincide very nicely.

75

I tagged along a few times with the British artist Foster Spragge while she was working on a walking and mapping project titled 'Drawing Dialogues on the London Loop'. She was conducting a 150-mile walk around the outskirts of the city, divided into fifteen separate walks. I went with her from Uxbridge to Moor Park, on another occasion from Rainham to Purfleet, and once along the canal from Richmond; just a fraction of the whole.

Foster carried with her a clipboard on which was a sheet of paper, marked up with a line of dots and holes. Every seven minutes as we walked, she used a compass embedded in a clear plastic ruler with two circular holes in it (a nautical device) and centred it on the spot marked by a hole, drew a line marking the east/ west axis, and then drew a couple of circles. I admit that I didn't understand the fine details of this process. We agreed that it would be possible to use the resulting map to, as it were, reverse engineer the route, but I don't imagine anybody ever did that. The end result was a set of gorgeously inscrutable images that were later shown in a library in Westminster.

As we walked, we occasionally met and shared a few words with other walkers, including a photographer who was looking for fly agaric mushrooms which he'd seen growing nearby the previous year when he hadn't had his camera with him. Now he wanted to photograph one of these mighty mushrooms in order for it to be used on a Christmas card. But we never met anybody who asked what we were doing. This surprised me at first, and I thought it would have been interesting to show them Foster's complex and inscrutable images and get some instant feedback, but none of the people we passed or encountered ever showed any curiosity about us and our activities. Eventually we put it down to the clipboard. It made Foster look like she might be, not an artist but a local government official conducting some kind of survey. Nobody wants to get too involved with something like that.

76

There's a tried and, to some extent trusted, 'experimental' walking technique that involves using a map of one place while walking in a completely different place. I'm never sure quite how I feel about this. I mean it seems sort of interesting, but when you arrive at the first river or dead end that isn't on your map, then surely the conceit and the fun ends pretty abruptly. Looking for the Eiffel Tower in Stoke-on-Trent isn't really all that fascinating an enterprise.

Then I found an example of this kind of thing in a surprising place – in Evelyn Waugh's travel book *Labels: A Mediterranean Journey* (1930). It's his account of the Mediterranean cruise he took the previous year with his wife, also named Evelyn. One of the places they visited was Malta, and Waugh bought himself a guidebook titled *Walks in Malta* by one F. Weston, published by the

Daily Malta Chronicle, Valetta. Secondhand copies are surprisingly expensive to come by.

Waugh reports that he enjoyed the book because of its stern and terse instructions to sightseers, 'Turning sharply to your left you will notice ...' etc. On one occasion when using the book, Waugh ended up at the Senglea Quay, but he thought it was Vittoriosa, and walked on for some time in the wrong town, being instructed to notice 'windows with fine old mouldings,' 'partially defaced escutcheons,' 'interesting iron-work balustrades,' etc. It was only when he was instructed to observe an obviously non-existent cathedral that he realised where he'd gone wrong.

Most of us, without calling ourselves experimental walkers, have done something similar on our travels, looked for the right thing in the wrong place, found we were trying to make sense of the wrong page of the map. Often it feels simply annoying, sometimes we see the funny side, like Waugh, and sometimes it results in a walk in places we'd never have found in normal circumstances, if we'd had the 'proper' guide. I suppose once in a while we might also experience a Debordian derangement of the senses.

77

For what it's worth, I too have been a tourist in Malta, with my first wife shortly after we were married. She wasn't strictly speaking a tourist since she'd previously lived there for a while. Her father had been in the British Navy and was stationed there, so she knew parts of the island pretty well. I had certainly read Thomas Pynchon's *V.* at the time, but like a fool I didn't use it to inform my visit to Malta. And I don't remember us having either a map or a guidebook, though surely we must have. I do remember we bought a book on Maltese cooking, but that can't have been much help.

So then when I got home, I reread parts of *V.* I don't know if Pynchon is or was much of a flâneur, but it's not hard to imagine him as a young man in the navy, an aspiring writer, drifting through the streets of Valetta some time in the 1950s, consulting an old Baedeker as he went.

There's a relevant passage in *V.*, chapter 11, 'Confessions of Fausto Maijstral', describing Valletta in a blackout during the German bombardment. I suppose a map's no use in a blackout even if it's of the right place. Pynchon writes, 'The street of the 20th Century, at whose far end or turning – we hope – is some sense of home or safety. But no guarantees. A street we are put at the wrong end of, for reasons best known to the agents who put us there. But a street we must walk.'

Probably it would have been no bad thing to have a map as you walked the street of the twentieth century, but there would surely be many competing and often misguided versions, many of them containing false or mistaken contradictory information. Is that better or worse than having no map at all?

78

I'm not a Pynchon scholar by any means, but I am an enthusiast. I went walking in Manhattan Beach because I'd found the address where Pynchon lived in the 1960s and early '70s. I wandered into the Bradbury Building in downtown LA for various reasons, but not least because it appears in *Gravity's Rainbow* and *Against the Day*. And I walked around White Sands in New Mexico, a national park and a missile range, because it's home to a couple of German V-2s which feature so front and centre in *Gravity's Rainbow*.

And that's why I went for a walk along Staveley Road, Chiswick, London W4, built in the late 1920s and early 1930s, because it's where the first V-2 flying bomb landed in England. The V-2 was both a rocket and a ballistic missile, a successor to the V-1, but whereas the V-1 flew at subsonic speeds, the V-2 flew faster than the speed of sound. You could hear the V-1 coming, and when the engine cut out you knew it was on its way down, but you still had time to run, or even possibly walk, to a shelter. However, since the V-2 was supersonic you heard the explosion and then, if you were lucky, if you'd survived, you heard the sound of it approaching. This idea plays a crucial part in *Gravity's Rainbow*, where Pynchon turns it into a Pavlovian metaphor for the disconnection between cause and effect.

That first V-2 landed and exploded at about a quarter to seven on 8 September 1944 in Staveley Road. We know for certain that three people were killed instantly: Rosemary Clarke who was a child of three, Ada Harrison a woman in her sixties who lived at number 3, and Sapper Bernard Browning, who was walking down the street on his way to Chiswick Station, to catch a train to go and meet his girlfriend.

Information surrounding the event is remarkably inconsistent. The age of Ada Harrison for example comes in somewhere between sixty-three and sixty-eight. The reason I wrote 'about a quarter to seven' as the time of the explosion, is because the exact time quoted varies depending on the source. Some sources can't even decide whether it was the morning or the evening, though the vast majority go for the former. You may learn that nineteen people were injured, or perhaps eleven or twenty-two. Sources will tell you that six houses, or eleven or eighteen, were completely destroyed and another six or fifteen or twenty-seven severely damaged, some of them so badly (I don't know how many) that they had to be demolished for safety reasons.

The government of the day has some responsibility for the lack of clarity, done in the name of keeping up wartime morale. The official story was that a gas main had exploded, though of course the locals knew better. Churchill didn't publicly acknowledge the existence of the V-2 until early November. Events in Staveley Road were a sign of things to come. In due course over 2,500 British civilians were killed in V-2 attacks, and about 6,500 were injured.

I knew there was a monument in Staveley Road marking that first V-2 attack. Given that it was in deepest suburbia, I wasn't expecting anything very extreme or avant-garde, but I was expecting a little more than I found. The monument was, is, a black granite block, perhaps two feet tall and fifteen inches square, the top sloping down from the rear to the front. And it had an inscription, all capitals, 'In memory of all V-2 attack victims', with the Battlefield Trust insignia etched into the granite. A modest piece then, made more modest still by its sitting on a tiny patch of ground in front of an electricity substation with two mysterious mechanical lumps sitting on it.

However, thinking about it later, it occurred to me that perhaps the street itself and its continuing existence is a kind of monument. Clearly it doesn't look the way it did in 1944, but it was instructive to look at the older houses and see that no two of them currently look exactly alike. There are the usual variations you find in any suburb; replacement doors and windows, new porches, garages and extensions, loft conversions, but here it seemed more significant. Here you'd have a hard time telling which houses date from the original development, and which ones were built or rebuilt after the war, so it became a monument to endurance and healing, a walk-through monument to itself.

79

My grandfather, who joined the army as a volunteer during the First World War at the age of fourteen, often used to say, 'You never hear the bullet that kills you.' He spent the Second World War as a civilian in Sheffield and I never heard him mention V-1s or V-2s – they never got as far north as Sheffield – but he did used to say, 'If a bomb's got your name on it there's nothing you can do about it.' He'd lost an eye during his time in the army, though whether to a bullet or a bomb or something else, was never discussed.

I keep thinking about Sapper Bernard Browning, killed in that first Staveley Road V-2 attack. In fact, he lived round the corner in Elmwood Road, but the obvious and most convenient walking route to the station took him along Staveley Road. If he'd walked a different route, or if he'd set off a few minutes earlier or later, he'd most likely have avoided the V-2. You could use this to confirm or contradict my grandfather's wisdom. But whether that bomb had his name on it or not, we can be sure that as he was walking along, probably thinking about his girlfriend whom he was on the way to meet, he definitely never heard it coming.

80

The first time I went to London I was sixteen years old. It was for a long weekend, going down from Sheffield with my parents and some family friends. We were complete rubes. We didn't know what anything was or where it was, and we didn't even particularly know what we wanted to see or do. We knew the names of some familiar places: Greenwich, Birdcage Walk, the Tower of London, and we went to all of them. We walked ourselves into the ground. And somehow – I think it must have been after we'd taken a boat ride along the Thames – we ended up walking around the Southbank, including the exterior of the Hayward Gallery, which I now know had only been completed the previous year.

I liked the Hayward because it seemed new and modern and different, though I certainly had no idea the architectural style was called Brutalism, whether old or new. My dad, on the other hand, was horrified by the architecture. He was a joiner, and by then a foreman for the council on various building sites around Sheffield. He looked at the finish of the Hayward, with the impressions of wood grain in the concrete, and what he saw was 'shuttering', familiar enough from his own job: wooden planks used to create a form that was filled with concrete, when you were making a foundation or a trench. It was the kind of work you gave to joiners who turned up at the site and weren't skilled enough to do anything else. The idea that you'd leave this visible on the outside of a finished building was just incomprehensible to him.

There was an exhibition of Pop Art on at the Hayward when we were there, and I really wanted to go in, but I couldn't tempt any of the others. We walked on.

One way or another I've spent a fair amount of time over the years walking in and around the Hayward, going to exhibitions, even working there very briefly as a gallery attendant. And during a particularly grim period when I taught creative writing to fashion students in Epsom (yes, really), I used to go there after work in an attempt to decompress. Somewhere along the line, I did realise, having read my Reyner Banham, that this was indeed an example of Brutalism, possibly even New Brutalism.

At the time of that first visit, I knew very little about Pop Art, or anything else, but I was aware of Andy Warhol. It was the start of a long interest. A couple of years later I was watching *Flesh* and *Trash*, and when I got to university there was *Chelsea Girls* and *Lonesome Cowboys*, and eventually *Empire* and *Sleep*, but a lot had happened, both to me and to Warhol, by then.

81

I first set foot in New York City, specifically Manhattan, in the late 1970s not long after I'd finished university. I was smart enough in certain respects, devastatingly naive in others. As evidence of the latter, I thought the obvious thing to do while in New York was to drop in on good old Andy Warhol. He'd obviously be delighted to make the acquaintance of some complete stranger from England who had a genuine, if unsophisticated, enthusiasm for his work, both paintings and films.

A quick look in the Yellow Pages (remember them?) gave me the address of Andy Warhol Enterprises. I believe it was 860 Broadway, though I just found this by doing an online search rather than because it's indelibly etched in my memory. I walked down there, stood outside the building, seriously intending to go in, but ultimately, I couldn't bring myself to do it. I was too shy, too unsure of myself, too socially awkward, and I chickened out. I walked away from the building, trying not to feel too much like an idiot and a loser.

In retrospect I'm sure it was very much for the best that I didn't go in. People who know about these things assure me I'd never have got past reception. This was well after Warhol had been shot by Valerie Solanas, and strangers were not embraced the way they had been back in the early 1960s. In any case I doubt that I'd have been clasped to the extended Warhol bosom. I had youth on my side, but I'm sure I didn't have what the Warhol crew was looking for. I wasn't cool, wild, druggy, dangerous looking, sexually ambiguous. What chance would I have had?

New York at that time was a bracingly scary place to go walking – muggings, prostitutes in hot pants, genuinely dangerous looking men offering drugs that they might or might not actually have. A stroll in Central Park was reputed to be a suicide mission. This, I suppose, was Warhol's New York, and I was happy to walk in it, but back then I couldn't have told you where Warhol lived or ate or hung out. I certainly had no idea which church he attended, or that he went to church at all.

All this information is now easily available from various sources. There's even a book by Thomas Kiedrowski titled *Andy Warhol's New York City: Four*

Walks, Uptown to Downtown. From time to time, I've found myself wishing I had a time machine so I could take this walking guide and go back the necessary number of decades. I might still not be welcomed by the Warhol crew, but I'm a good deal less shy and socially awkward now than I was then, and at least I'd know where to walk in order to engineer a 'chance' encounter with Andy, Edie, Viva, Mary Woronov or whoever.

82

The fact is, Warhol does seem to have been a walker. Photographs by Ron Galella, who to a large extent was Warhol's own personal paparazzo, confirm this. There are other confirmations, such as an interview by Claire Demers, which appeared in the summer 1977 issue of *Christopher Street* magazine. Mostly Demers asks Warhol how he feels about New York, and he says, 'Oh, yes, I like walking the best.'

Did he really like walking best? Honestly? Better than art, better than celebrity, better than voyeurism, better than going to parties, better than cake? It seems unlikely, and from his diaries you might think Warhol spent most of his time in cabs and limos, or in the Rolls Royce he owned.

And yet there's footage on YouTube that proves he was a walker. You can find him there walking along, one hand holding a dog leash attached to his pet dog, in the other a small camera, a Minox, I think. He certainly couldn't have walked through New York discreetly, even when somebody wasn't filming him, but then discretion was not really his thing. A lot of people would have known who he was, and even if by some chance they didn't, they'd surely have stared at this odd-looking man in a bad wig.

Two people I knew – Adam Alexander a mathematical prodigy who invented the Alexander Star, a variation on the Rubik's cube, and his wife Leslie Sternbergh an illustrator and graphic artist – had an encounter with Warhol while walking in the East Village where they lived and were minor celebrities. They were startling looking people, very sharply dressed. Adam had long, long grey hair, and Lesley had long, long red hair. You couldn't help noticing them if you saw them in the street and on this occasion, they were noticed by Warhol, who stopped them and took a few photographs of them with the camera he was carrying, this time a Polaroid. He snapped away, maybe half a dozen times, and Lesley asked if they could have one of the resulting pictures. Since every Polaroid is unique, they would have owned an original Warhol. But Warhol wasn't giving his art away to people he just happened to have noticed while walking.

83

I find the idea of 'Warhol's New York' simultaneously very attractive and rather absurd. As modern tourism becomes ever more pervasive and (for want of a better word) inventive, there's a small industry providing walking tours that enable you to see places through the eyes (or at least personal habits) of ever more historic, literary or artistic figures. The overheads are attractively low. In Manhattan, you can walk with Salinger, in Brooklyn with Walt Whitman. Graffiti or street art walking tours currently seem to be popular. In London it's Dickens, William Blake, Sherlock Holmes, Karl Marx, and a slew of others. In Paris you can follow in the footsteps of Sartre or Toulouse Lautrec, and of any number of American artistic expats. You can certainly walk in Guy Debord's footsteps: there are details online, though it seems to me that he really didn't get around all that much.

New York, London, Paris – these cities are big enough that multiple views and versions are possible. New York does not only belong to Warhol, much less Salinger. London is not solely Dickensian. But what about those places with a single, or at least an overwhelming, presence? Joyce in Dublin, Kafka in Prague, Jane Austen in Bath, Dali in Port Lligat. You wouldn't want to be the *other* painter in Giverny, the other literary presence in Faulkner's Oxford, Mississippi. If you're a playwright, you surely couldn't live in Shakespeare's Stratford. However, I admit that I'm a bit of a sucker for this stuff. I'm a man who absolutely had to go to Barstow, for no other reason than it's mentioned in the opening line of Hunter S. Thompson's *Fear and Loathing in Las Vegas*. I made a long diversion to Coxwold in North Yorkshire because that's where Lawrence Sterne had lived, worked and walked.

I've enjoyed myself well enough on my excursions to these places, but I do realise that in the end there's something unsatisfying, and even indeed reductive, about this kind of pilgrimage. You can't *really* walk in Raymond Chandler's Los Angeles or on the banks of Thomas Cole's Hudson River – though I've tried to do both – because essentially these places are inventions, artistic creations. They exist sure enough, but they exist on the page or on canvas and, of course, in the mind and imagination of the reader or viewer. Ultimately, they're no more 'real' than Calvino's invisible cities.

The great places belong to everybody and to nobody. That's their appeal. You don't have to write a book or create a painting to make a place yours. Simply walking through it may be enough.

84

When Norman Mailer ran for mayor of New York in 1969, his plans included free public bicycles, no private cars allowed in Manhattan (he, of course, conveniently lived in Brooklyn), and one day a month called 'Sweet Sunday' when all mechanical transportation, public or private, and including elevators (and I suppose bicycles since they're mechanical) would be banned. I imagine a lot of walking would have been involved. It all sounds very unlikely to have been embraced by the population of New York, and of course the chances of Mailer getting elected were minimal, though he did win a surprisingly creditable 5 per cent of the vote.

Warhol and Mailer were hardly soul brothers, though they sometimes moved in the same circles. In the movie, *Factory Girl*, about Edie Sedgwick, there's a scene where Andy Warhol (played by Guy Pierce) goes to see his priest and confesses that he's envious of his friend Mark who was at a party on Cape Cod when Mailer walked up and punched him in the stomach. Warhol was there too and wishes Mailer had walked up and punched *him* in the stomach.

This seems to have been more or less true. The punchee was Mark Lancaster, and Mailer apparently called him a 'pansy effete Englishman' before punching him. Warhol however didn't wait to go to confession to deliver his lines about being envious; he said it publicly at the time, at the party, as a camp put down of Mailer's 'manliness'. And in fact, I don't doubt that Norman Mailer would have been more than happy to walk over and punch Warhol too, but perhaps he didn't want to give him the satisfaction.

85

In the last week of his life Andy Warhol took two very significant walks. He was registered with the Ford Modeling Agency, and they got him a gig for Tuesday 17 February 1987 for a fashion show at the club Tunnel where he modelled clothes designed by Kohshin Satoh. Also modelling was Miles Davis. Warhol strutted his stuff, and the crowd loved it, but Warhol wasn't so happy about it.

Afterwards he complained to his diary that they had designed a $5000-custom outfit for Miles with gold notes on it, while he looked like the poor stepchild, 'and in the end they told me I walked too slow.'

There was a good reason for that slowness. Warhol was in a lot of pain and had been for a while because of an ongoing bladder condition. Four days after the fashion show he walked into New York Hospital, accompanied by Ken Laland, an assistant he sometime referred to as his 'walker'. He was going in for gallbladder surgery and was considered an 'ambulatory emergency patient', a walk-in.

He never walked out of the hospital and died in his bed two days later. The circumstances of his death were, of course, dreadful, much contested and resulted in an out of court malpractice settlement. Still, his last public appearance, his last public walk, was at a fashion show, on stage with Miles Davis. Not too shabby.

86

You know, for all that Andy Warhol is considered to be a 'gay icon', it was the women in Warhol's films that first really grabbed my attention: Edie Sedgwick, Ultra Violet, Nico, Mary Woronov. They looked fabulous, like nobody I'd ever met, and of course I knew that in the real world they'd never give me the time of day, but then a lot of the women I met in the real world wouldn't give me the time of day in any case. Better to be rejected by a superstar than some girl from the local comprehensive school.

Watching Warhol's films, I could just about put up with the antics of Ondine, Taylor Mead, Gerard Malanga et al, as long as I got to see the wonderful women.

When I lived in Los Angeles I did briefly make friends with Mary Woronov, star of *Chelsea Girls* among other Warhol films, and also star of far more non-Warhol films, including *Death Race 2000* and *Eating Raoul*. Knowing her wasn't exactly a dream come true, but it did confirm that I was no longer the shy, social inadequate lad I'd been back in the day in New York. She and I had done a reading together, had both had a bad experience with the same English publisher, and in the literary world that's enough to establish a friendship. It was no big deal. We had coffee together, then lunch, and we talked about things, though only very rarely about Warhol. She wasn't eager, and I didn't press her.

On one occasion I walked the couple of miles from my home to the coffee shop where we were meeting. This surprised and impressed her, and she offered to give me a ride home. I was too star-struck to refuse. As we walked to her car, a RAV 4 as I remember, she gave me a considered look, and said, unprompted, 'Oh, that's a good walk you have there. That's a very nice stride.' I smiled fit to burst. I'm not sure I necessarily want that emblazoned on my tombstone, but I wouldn't mind having it on a tee-shirt.

87

If you're unimpressed by that, you're certainly going to be unimpressed by this.

As is well known, towards the end of 1974 Werner Herzog learned that Lotte Eisner, the French–German film critic and curator, was gravely ill and likely to die. Herzog set off walking from Munich, where he lived, to Paris where Lotte Eisner lived, 'In full faith, believing she would stay alive if I came on foot.' These words are from the introduction to *Of Walking in Ice*, the book he wrote describing the walk. It was a hard journey, but it apparently worked. Lotte Eisner lived for another eight years. Now, although a lot of people may imagine that Herzog lives in a cave in the mountains or a tent at the edge of some blasted plain, I discovered that in fact he was living in a very pleasant suburban spread in Los Angeles. I even knew the address. And it so happened that a new edition of one of my books about walking was going to be published, and I wanted a few juicy blurbs for the cover. What could be better than a quotation from Werner Herzog?

I got a copy of the earlier edition of my book and put it in an envelope with a note asking politely for this favour, saying that 'in full faith', I believed he would give me a blurb if I came on foot. And I walked the seven miles from my house to his and put the book in his mailbox. Naturally, I never heard from him.

However, I can say that I did once walk with Werner Herzog. It was at a lunch party in Ventura County, north of Los Angeles, at a grand house belonging to a German publisher – not his only house by any means. There were a few celebrities there but also plenty of civilians and everybody talked to everybody else. When lunch was over, we all went out into the garden and I found myself walking with Werner Herzog from the house to the swimming pool. It was a biggish garden, though not huge. The walk may have been thirty yards long. Herzog had, of course, noticed that I was English, and attempting to make conversation, he said he thought that former Prime Minister John Major was a much underrated politician. I was left speechless by this, and I certainly didn't mention that I was the weirdo who'd walked to his house and left him a note begging for a blurb.

88

When I lived in New York, a good while after the death of Warhol, I was persuaded to interview the photographer Peter Beard 'on stage' in a bookshop in New York. The truth was I knew very little about Beard at the time. I knew he had some connection with Warhol and owned a property next door to him in Montauk. I knew he photographed wildlife and fashion models, was an old Africa hand and had been a confidante of Karen Blixen, but that really didn't amount to much.

In the event, my ignorance was of no great consequence. Beard was absolutely the easiest man to interview. Any question, whether about Africa or Warhol, Blixen or the elephant that gored him, produced a long, articulate and highly opinionated answer. I could just have held up flash cards. I now realise I should have asked him about walking, because he was obviously something of a walker. He was known to his friends as Walkabout for his tendency to wander off on adventures. But one thing I did notice about him on that occasion, although he didn't seem to have any difficulty walking, was that his feet were strangely swollen and misshapen, and he wore big soft sandals to accommodate them. I probably wouldn't have mentioned that even if I had asked him about walking.

In 2020, he wandered off from his home in Montauk and went missing, but at first nobody was very concerned. His disappearance was reported in the papers but to an outsider it looked as if he was off on another of his adventures. However, in due course we learned that he'd been diagnosed with dementia, and we know that wandering is a symptom of that disease. The people I talked to about it at the time suggested that, aware of his condition, he might have decided to end it all by walking into the sea – a very brave and elegant way to go, which would have been typical of the man. But, in fact, no, he simply walked into the woods and got lost, where he was found dead not so very much later, by a hunter.

89

It was in Peter Beard's book *The End of the Game*, 1965, that I first read about Ewart S. Grogan, 1874–1967, who, newly graduated from Cambridge, fell in love and wanted to marry Gertrude Watt, the sister of a Cambridge friend. But Gertrude's stepfather wasn't sure that Grogan had the right stuff. So Grogan said, 'What if I walked from Cape Town to Cairo?', a thing nobody had ever done at the time, and the stepfather said, 'All right then.' So off he went, in 1898. When I say nobody had ever done it, I mean that Grogan was the first European, although I don't imagine that many, if any, native Africans had been crazy enough to attempt it either.

Grogan completed his walk, but not without some help. Along the way he suffered from a fever, and a hideous-sounding foot injury received while elephant-hunting. He had to be carried. So although he 'walked the length of Africa,' he was carried for some of it by his porters, who were obviously walking, although none of them stayed with him from the beginning to the end of the journey, so none of them got to say they'd walked the length of Africa either.

Grogan lived until 1967, and Beard met him. It's strange to think that a man who fought in the Matabele Wars, lived long enough that he could meet a friend of Andy Warhol.

90

There's a caricature by 'Ape' from Vanity Fair, showing Verney Lovett Cameron (1844–1894), captioned 'He Walked Across Africa'. Cameron did it a different way from Grogan, going from east to west. In 1875, he arrived in Zanzibar intending to assist Dr Livingstone, but by the time he got there Livingstone was dead, so Cameron pressed on, intending to explore the main stream of the Congo River, but he couldn't obtain canoes so he continued on foot.

He was certainly the first European to cross Equatorial Africa from sea to shining sea – Zanzibar in the east to Benguella in the west (sometimes spelled Benguela), but again it wasn't absolutely straightforward. Cameron's diary from April 1873, extracted in his book *Across Africa*, tells us that he was in so much pain that he could neither walk nor ride and had to be carried in a hammock. In other words, he didn't really walk all the way across Africa, either.

91

If you're looking for a European walker in Africa, it's hard to ignore Sir Richard Francis Burton. Among many, many other things, he was the translator of the first 'erotic' book I ever read, *The Perfumed Garden*. It was passed around at my school and was reckoned to be very hot stuff, though much of it went a long way over my head, and long stretches were not very erotic at all. Taking a look at it now, with an emphasis on walking, I find this, in the chapter 'Concerning Women Who Deserve to be Praised': 'When she is walking, her natural parts appear as set off under clothing.' I'm not sure I know what that means even now.

Walking was the very least of what Burton got up to in Africa and elsewhere, but his books provide plenty of details of the journeys he took on foot. This is from *First Footsteps in East Africa*, published in 1856. 'At daybreak

I set out with four Arab matchlock-men, and taking a direction nearly due west, waded and walked over an alluvial plain flooded by every high tide. On our way we passed lines of donkeys and camels carrying water-skins from the town; they were under guard like ourselves, and the sturdy dames that drove them indulged in many a loud joke at our expense.' Ah, those loud, sturdy, joking women.

Later that same morning, after another walk, Burton continues:

Returning, we breakfasted in the garden, and rain coming on, we walked out to enjoy the Oriental luxury of a wetting. Ali Iskandar, an old Arab mercenary, afforded us infinite amusement: a little opium made him half crazy, when his sarcastic pleasantries never ceased.

Ah yes, who doesn't enjoy the sarcastic pleasantries of an opium addict when out for a walk?

92

'When at night I walk barefoot in my sandals across fields of snow at the Austrian border, I shall not flinch ... I project myself to the mind's heaven.'

That's Jean Genet in *The Thief's Journal*. Good stuff, I thought when I first read it, but then I shared it with a few people, one of whom said, 'Well, how can you be barefoot if you're walking in sandals?' She had a point. I assume that Genet meant that he was sockless, but 'sockless' doesn't sound at all poetic, and using his logic you could surely be barefoot in your socks. In fact, aren't we all barefoot in our socks or tights or stockings? Anyway, it probably pays not to be too literal when it comes to Genet.

Genet makes an appearance in Kathy Acker's novel *Blood and Guts in High School*. I don't know if Acker was much of a walker. I did find some footage of her walking in the lower East Side in Manhattan, from a 1984 South Bank Show, but there are far more pictures that show her in the gym or on a motorcycle. These things are not, I accept, mutually exclusive.

Walking crops up in more or less interesting ways in the book, when for instance, in Manhattan, Janey, the book's heroine and Acker's alter ego, 'walks up and down the same street as the hookers walk only the hookers make some money.' Am I being a complete spoilsport if I point out that it isn't the walking that makes them money?

Then Janey is in Tangier and, lo and behold, she sees Jean Genet walking along the street. Despite being warned that he has a reputation for being aloof and difficult, she decides she *must* talk to him, which she does, and Genet is unexpectedly charmed by her. She quotes him in her diary as saying, 'Loneliness and poverty made me not walk but fly.'

I find it hard to believe that Acker was ever, in the ordinary sense, lonely, and her financial arrangements were extremely unclear; we know she had a trust fund and was able to buy a flat in London, despite a much professed lack of funds. She also said she couldn't afford medical insurance.

In fact, it seems that Acker really did meet Genet, introduced to him by William Burroughs (of course), though that doesn't have much to do with what happens in her novel. Janey sees Genet again, they decide to travel together and after many difficulties and much experimental prose they end up in the desert outside Alexandria. 'The desert is absolutely brilliant', says Janey.

Towards the end of their entanglement Genet tells her to get some sleep. 'Sleep,' she says, 'If I'm walking across rocks ... it's murder to my everlasting sleep.' When they get to Luxor, Genet gives her money, abandons her and goes off to see a production of one of his plays. The literary result of this, as described in Acker's text, is simply: 'She dies.' Well, who doesn't?

93

I don't know that Genet was much more of a pedestrian than Acker, but I do know he was briefly besotted with an eighteen-year-old tightrope walker named Abdallah Bentaga, and eventually he wrote a short text titled *The Tightrope Walker* (*Le Funambule*). It contains the line 'wire will carry you better, more surely than a road.'

This was written with irony and hindsight. Genet paid for Bentaga to have high wire lessons, but Bentaga fell and destroyed his knee, ending his tightrope walking career. Genet then bought him what's referred to in various sources as a 'small circus'. Sometimes I think, 'We should all have such lovers,' but then I'm not so sure. Owning a circus of whatever size must be quite a liability.

After a while Genet started seeing somebody else, so Bentaga killed himself by slitting his wrists. Genet said he'd never write again, but being a writer, he did.

94

I never met Kathy Acker, but I've known quite a few people who did. The general feeling, as expressed to me, was that she was trouble, and some found her too much trouble. She suggested to my ex-wife, who was also a gym enthusiast, and had been the editor of a motorcycle magazine (under a male pseudonym), that they team up and cruise the bars of Lower Manhattan picking up boys. My ex-wife declined.

Acker died in 1997, aged fifty, after what is often called 'a battle with cancer'. I'm battling it right now as I sit here, pen in one hand, glass of Merlot nearby. You fight your battles your way, I'll fight my battles my way.

Acker was diagnosed with breast cancer in 1996 and had a double mastectomy, and then elected, against medical advice, not to have chemotherapy. According to her own account, and that of Charles Shaar Murray, her boyfriend at the time, chemo would only have increased her survival chances by about ten per cent. Murray reports that she told him to leave her and find somebody new, that he shouldn't waste his time with a 'walking dead woman'.

I can well understand why Acker wouldn't want to put herself through the ordeal of chemotherapy. However, I find her desire to put herself in the hands of quacks after her rejection of 'western medicine' less comprehensible. In an article titled 'The Gift of Disease' (Acker was always good with titles), she wrote: 'The hardest part of my cancer was walking away from that surgeon and from conventional medicine.' In Acker's case it was also to walk into a zone populated by faith healers, card readers, astrologers and psychics. Acker's psychic told her she was going to be just fine.

Eventually Acker went to Tijuana hoping to receive treatment at the Gerson Institute, an alternative cancer treatment centre based on the work of Max B. Gerson, considered to be a complete charlatan by most, although his followers revere him as a misunderstood genius conspired against by the forces of convention.

The staff at the Institute wouldn't take Acker because they saw that the cancer was too advanced. She ended up at a place called American Biologics, a different alternative, favoured by the Amish and Mennonites. It's not clear to me whether American Biologics is still in business, although until recently there was a website with that name that said they were an 'integrated facility' offering 'a wide variety of approaches, including laetrile, enzymes, chelation, oxygen therapies, bioelectrical therapies, nutritional therapy, hydrotherapy, and hyperthermia.'

It may not come as a great surprise that these treatments did not cure Kathy Acker's cancer. The gap between the original diagnosis and her death was about eighteen months.

95

To abandon conventional medicine is, I suppose, to wish for a miracle, something any of us might do at one time or another. If the doctors say they can't cure you, you might as well try something else, anything else.

My own father, having retired from work, but still doing some jobbing carpentry, found he was having terrible back pain. He had trouble walking and eventually he needed help even to lift up his toolbox to get it in or out of his car. He consulted his own doctor who wasn't much help, but said the pain was mechanical in origin, so in desperation my dad had a session with an acupuncturist. The pain felt worse after the acupuncture than before, but in his desperation, he took this as a sign the acupuncturist must be onto something, at least operating in the right area, perhaps thinking that some things have to get worse before they get better.

The back pain was eventually diagnosed as renal cancer. He never walked anywhere again, and he was dead within two months. I'm very glad he didn't embrace quackery even if conventional medicine didn't seem to do him much good. I also remember, with a lot of ambivalence, something a nurse at my dad's hospital said to my mother, 'There are worse things than cancer, you know.'

96

All of which makes me think of Garry Winogrand, one of my favorite photographers. He hated the term 'street photographer', but most people would think that's precisely what he was. The thing about street photographers is that they walk the streets and end up taking lots of pictures of other people who are also walking the streets. I find this enormously appealing. I've never had serious ambitions to be a 'real' photographer. I never fantasised about being a fashion photographer or a war photographer, but once in a while I've fantasised about being a street photographer, like Winogrand, Cartier-Bresson, Lee Friedlander, Vivian Maier, Diane Arbus. It's a genre that allows, in fact demands, that the photographer does a lot of walking.

Winogrand was a New Yorker through and through, who grew up in the Bronx, and I think it's fair to say, even though he took pictures in many parts of America and elsewhere, that the majority of his best pictures were taken in New York.

At the beginning of the 1980s, which turned out to be towards the end of his life, he moved to Los Angeles and took a lot of pictures there too. By then, however, he wasn't doing much walking. He was suffering from thyroid issues, he was hampered by a slow-to-heal broken leg, and his personal life was a mess. This inevitably changed his way of working. He spent a lot of time being driven around LA, often by his printer Tom Consilvio, shooting relentlessly out of the car windows, sometimes apparently at random, not bothering to focus, not caring to hold the camera steady or even apparently having a subject in mind. This does not sound like the very best way to take photographs, certainly not 'street photographs', and the received wisdom is that it indicated a great falling off in the quality of Winogrand's work. This is an occasion when the received wisdom appears to be essentially, if not absolutely, true. I think there are few great pictures from that era.

John Szarkowski wrote in the catalogue for a 1988 exhibition that Winogrand 'photographed whether or not he had anything to photograph, and that he photographed most when he had no subject, in the hope that the act of photographing might lead him to one.'

This sounds to me like a possible response to artistic block, but it's still not separable from the sense that Winogrand had, in some sense, 'lost it' and being an obsessive, he was working obsessively to 'find it' again.

In interviews earlier in his life, Winogrand famously said that he photographed things 'to see what they looked like photographed', but there was now a contradiction. He photographed things, but no longer seemed to care what they looked like. He left behind him a couple of thousand unprocessed films, and hundreds of thousands of unedited images.

Some of those who are sympathetic to Winogrand's late work, and I'm one of them, will say that he was deliberately testing the boundaries of what constitutes a photograph, consciously subverting our notions of subject matter, what is 'worth' photographing and how a photograph should look. Others, even if they're sympathetic, think he simply knew it was over for him, both as an artist and as a human being. But one thing he apparently didn't know: he was about to be diagnosed with gallbladder cancer. And like Acker, whatever his reasons, he decided to reject conventional medicine and go to the Gerson Clinic in Tijuana, the very place that would later reject Acker for being too far gone. They were happy enough to accept Winogrand. He died four and a half weeks later.

97

I tried to love *The Walking Dead*, the AMC zombie apoc-
alypse TV series based on the comic book by Robert
Kirkman, art by Tony Moore and Charlie Adlard. The
zombies in the show were known as 'walkers' which was
kind of cool, although most of them were walking very
badly, limping and staggering, as zombies tend to do.
And yes, walking zombies are a frightening thing, but
zombies driving buses or flying planes are far scarier, if
you ask me.

I did like the paradox inherent in the title. Walking
and being dead do seem to be antithetical, although we
know that in myth, legend and Shakespeare's *Hamlet* this
isn't the case, that the dead walk. At least Hamlet's father
has returned with a piece of news, a revelation, whereas
most zombies are just planning to eat you, or parts of
you.

I'm not the first to wonder why zombies need to eat other people's brains. Or why they need to eat at all. What happens if they don't get these precious brains? Do they die? But they're dead already, so are they going to get more dead? And even if you say they're only semi-dead, they're obviously in a lot of pain, so wouldn't dying 'properly', once and for all, be a blessed relief? Could it be that they want to live, just so they can keep on walking?

98

I sometimes dream that I'm walking with my late father who's been miraculously restored to life. He's not a zombie in the dream: he looks and behaves very much as he did in real life. You might think there'd be something consoling about this, to have a parent back, however briefly, to share a little extra time. But in fact, it's never a consolation. Even in the dream I know that my father is really dead, and even as we walk together, I know he's going to have to die all over again; a prospect that is terrible for both of us.

99

As I write these words, my own cancer seems neither very real, nor very threatening. I realise of course this is illusory, that it's both. It's not a risk or a possibility, it's not something that might be coming to get me. It's already here. It's inside me. The doctors are treating it, and I'm doing what I can, doing what I'm told to do, but we all know there's only one possible outcome.

Would I complain if I died tomorrow? Would I feel cheated? Well, in the literal sense, no I wouldn't because I'd be dead, and I wouldn't be around to do any complaining. But even figuratively I wouldn't complain. I think I've had a good innings. My life hasn't been so bad and although I don't want it to end right now, I know it's going to end sooner rather than later, and although I'm not exactly happy about that, I'm accepting of it. That's the deal with mortality. That's the deal with being alive. How could you not accept it? Would you prefer to rage against the dying of the light? In what way is that better?

I'm not afraid of being dead, and I would say, even if I may be deceiving myself, that I never have been. On the other hand, I am very afraid indeed of pain. My current condition sometimes makes me feel deathly tired, my sleep is terrible, my appetite is shot, but I'm not in pain, not yet anyway.

I saw my father die in agony in hospital: they couldn't get the medication right. My mother on the other hand died alone in her own living room, while trying to get up from her chair one Saturday teatime to get to the fridge. I imagine she felt some pain, but it must have been very brief. Isn't that what we'd all settle for?

I know people say that some deaths are beautiful and peaceful, and take place in beautiful surroundings, with loved ones gathered at the bedside in fond attendance, but I have no direct, personal experience of that. I have, however, known people who've died in car crashes, one who died of an asthma attack, one in a skiing accident, one in an attack by muggers, and of course I've known some who've died of cancer. I've known people who've killed themselves. Two of these did involve walking. One went for a stroll by the golf course and slashed his wrists, another walked down to the railway line and lay down across the tracks until the train came. Suicides in the great outdoors seem always to be found by dog walkers.

Trying to decide what would be a fitting or appropriate death is a very bad and unwise idea. Dying while walking would be a fitting end for a man who's written about walking for so many years, but I'm sure that's far too neat, too much like literature, too much to ask for. Most of us die undramatic, unresonant deaths. Most of us die in beds, whether at home or in hospital. But even so I suppose there must always be a very last step, even if it's only a lurch from bed to wheelchair. If a journey of a thousand miles begins with a single step, then every journey, of whatever length, must also end with a single step. I wonder exactly where and when that step will be in my own case. I can't say I'm ready for it, but I think I'm as ready as I'll ever be.

And now it's time for me to go out for a walk. While I still can. No point in saying, 'I'll be back soon.'

ACKNOWLEDGEMENTS

Thanks and appreciation to all the following who have walked with me over greater or lesser distances, both physical and other (and thanks also to any that I may have missed):

Caroline Gannon
Anthony Miller
Ashley Biles
Lisa Jane Persky
Colin Marshall
Nicola Gray
Colin Samson
Penny Hughes-Stanton
Mel Thompson
Marianne Thompson
Jonathan Taylor
Sue Spooner
Paul Spooner
Mariette Rissenbeek
Robin Bell
Travis Elborough
Del Barrett
Jen Pedler
Richard Lapper
Loretta Ayeroff
Margaret Prescott
Chris Prescott
Susi Foxy Luard